# Physical Database Design for SYBASE® SQL Server™

# *Physical Database Design for SYBASE® SQL Server*™

## Rob Gillette, Dean Muench, Jean Tabaka

Prentice Hall PTR
Englewood Cliffs, NJ 07632

**Library of Congress Cataloging-In-Publication Data**

Gillette, Rob.
  Physical database design for SYBASE SQL Server / Rob Gillette,
Dean Muench, Jean Tabaka.
    p.  cm.
  Includes index.
  ISBN 0-13-161523-8
  1. Database design  2. Sybase.  3. SQL Server.  I. Muench, Dean.
II. Tabaka, Jean.  III. Title
QA76.9.D3G5235  1995
005.75'65—dc20                                        94-26912
                                                       CIP


*Editorial/production supervision:* BooksCraft, Inc., Indianapolis, IN
*Cover design:* Jeannette Jacobs
*Cover art:* Provided by Sybase, Inc.
*Interior design:* Shawn MacLaren
*Acquisitions editor:* Mark L. Taub
*Manufacturing manager:* Alexis R. Heydt

Published by Prentice Hall PTR
Prentice-Hall, Inc.
A Paramount Communications Company
Englewood Cliffs, NJ 07632

The publisher offers discounts on this book when ordered in bulk quantities. For more information contact:

  Corporate Sales Department
  Prentice Hall PTR
  113 Sylvan Avenue
  Englewood Cliffs, NJ 07632
  Phone: 201-592-2863
  FAX: 201-592-2249


Printed in the United States of America
10 9 8 7 6 5 4 3 2

ISBN 0-13-161523-8

Prentice-Hall International (UK) Limited, *London*
Prentice-Hall of Australia Pty. Limited, *Sydney*
Prentice-Hall Canada Inc., *Toronto*
Prentice-Hall Hispanoamericana, S.A., *Mexico*
Prentice-Hall of India Private Limited, *New Delhi*
Prentice-Hall of Japan, Inc., *Tokyo*
Simon & Schuster Asia Pte. Ltd., *Singapore*
Editora Prentice-Hall do Brasil, Ltda., *Rio de Janeiro*

# Acknowledgments

The authors gratefully acknowledge the valuable, professional assistance of the following contributors, technical reviewers, and editorial consultants:

Kevin Christopher, Marge duMond, Simon Keen, Monica Mehta, Karen Paulsell, Hal Spitz

The authors would also like to express thanks to the following individuals for their contributions:

Carmela Balassiano, Tarun Batra, Mark Christiansen, Charles Crafton, David Creighton, Chris Curvey, J. P. Dareys, Lisa DePascale, Mary Durham, Amram Dworkin, Christopher Eastman, Sylvain Gautier, Raj Gulati, Anita Heller, Tony Jarosz, Jeff Lichtman, JeanMarie Mariadassou, Dawn Melton, Howard Michalski, Bruce Miller, Stephen Morck, Murray Newcomb, Tom Oorebeek, Frank Pittelli, Ray Rankins, Steve Taylor, Royal Westwater, Chris Young.

# The Authors

Mr. Gillette, Mr. Muench, and Ms. Tabaka are members of the Methods & Tools group within Sybase Worldwide Professional Services. The mission of Methods & Tools is to deliver tools and publications supporting software engineering practice, project management, and client/server technology to both employees and customers of Sybase, Inc.

# Table of Contents

# *Figures*

# *Tables*

# *Preface*

*This practical guidebook is written to help database designers make the most of Sybase technology. The book focuses on Sybase-specific techniques and practices, helping you, the designer, to create a sound physical design for an SQL Server database to be used in the client/server architecture.*

The ordered steps in this book will guide you from the logical-design stage to an optimized physical design for single-server applications—where data is all in one location. Multiple-server database design, and other activities such as data distribution and replication, are not covered here.

## Who Should Use this Book

Experienced database designers who want to take full advantage of the capabilities and features of the SYBASE SQL Server—whether SQL Server 10.x or an earlier version—will refer to this book. This book is not a primer for people new to SQL Server, or new to database design; readers should have a general familiarity with both logical and physical design. The book is no substitute for documentation, education, and experience.

While not a project planning guide or a management handbook, the book will be helpful to project planners and quality managers as they oversee database-design projects.

## How to Use this Book

Use the book as a workbook. Its text and examples take you through a series of ordered activities and steps for choosing among alternative solutions for common situations. If you are new to physical database design, look over the Table of Contents before starting to carry out the activities, then perform the activities in order, reading through each chapter thoroughly before beginning the activity described therein.

You can also use the book as a quick reference guide, referring to the Table of Contents and the Index for pointers to chapters which hold specific information about database design. This works well when you have a completed design and, after some testing of your schema, you uncover a need for reworking of your physical design, whether because of a performance issue, a space issue, a security issue, or an integrity issue. Refer to the appropriate chapter in the book for quick answers to these specific problems.

Additionally, the organization of the book can be used by project planners and managers to develop tasking such as work breakdown structures based on the listed activities. Appendix D delineates the expected deliverables from the physical design process; this information can also be used in the project plan.

# Organization of the Book

To give you a sense of the flow of the physical-design process in the book, here is a brief description of the activity covered in each of the twenty-one chapters and four appendices:

1. **Defining Tables and Columns** — The initial transformation of the logical model into a physical model, including naming objects, choosing datatypes and lengths, and handling null values.

2. **Defining Keys** — Choosing primary and foreign keys, including the use of surrogate keys.

3. **Identifying Critical Transactions** — Identifying business transactions that are high-value, mission-critical, frequently performed, or costly in terms of computing resources.

4. **Adding Redundant Columns** — The first of a series of denormalization techniques: adding columns to tables that exist in other tables.

5. **Adding Derived Columns** — Adding a column to a table based on the values or existence of values in other columns in any table.

6. **Collapsing Tables** — Combining two or more tables into one table.

7. **Splitting Tables** — Partitioning a table into two or more disjoint tables. Partitioning may be horizontal (row-wise) or vertical (column-wise).

8. **Handling Supertypes and Subtypes** — Deciding how to implement tables that are involved in a supertype-subtype relationship in the logical model.

9. **Duplicating Parts of Tables** — Duplicating data vertically and/or horizontally into new tables.

10. **Adding Tables for Derived Data** — Creating new tables that hold data derived from columns in other tables.

11. **Handling Vector Data** — Deciding how to implement tables that contain plural attributes or vector data. Row-wise and column-wise implementations are discussed.

12. **Generating Sequence Numbers** — Choosing a strategy to generate sequence numbers, and the appropriate tables and columns to support the strategy.

13. **Specifying Indexes** — Specifying indexes to improve data access performance or to enforce uniqueness.

14. **Maintaining Row Uniqueness** — Maintaining the uniqueness of primary-key values.

15. **Handling Domain Restrictions** — Defining SQL Server rules and defaults on the columns of a table to maintain valid data values in columns.

16. **Handling Referential Integrity** — Deciding how to handle primary-key updates and deletes, and foreign-key inserts and updates. Using triggers to ensure referential integrity.

17. **Maintaining Derived and Redundant Data** — Specifying how data integrity will be maintained if the data model contains derived or redundant data.

18. **Handling Complex Integrity Constraints** — Deciding how to handle complex business rules such as sequence rules, cross-domain business rules, and complex data domain rules. Using triggers to implement complex business rules.

19. **Controlling Access to Data** — Restricting access to commands and data.

20. **Managing Object Sizes** — Calculating the estimated size of a database and its objects.

21. **Recommending Object Placement** — Allocating databases and their objects on available hardware to achieve optimal performance.

**Appendix A: The Sybase Development Framework and MethodSet** — Describes the development framework in which physical database design is performed.

**Appendix B: A Sample Database** — Provides a sample database model used for several logical and physical design examples throughout the book.

**Appendix C: Required Inputs to Physical Database Design** — Presents details about required preparation for the physical database design process.

**Appendix D: Physical Database Design Deliverables** — Lists the expected outcomes from the process.

**Appendix E: Naming Guidelines** — Suggests standards for naming objects on an SQL Server.

**Appendix F: Glossary** — Defines SYBASE SQL Server terms and relational database terms used in the book.

Each chapter of this book presents an activity or stage in your physical database design work.

■ To help you keep your bearings as you work through each stage, every chapter opens with a detailed introduction. This introduction first defines the activity, then tells you how to decide whether it is something you need to do.

■ Next comes a list of the things you need to have before you can start, a brief list of related issues (such as the need to revisit the activity later), and a numbered list of the tasks you will perform in the activity.

■ The body of the chapter presents detailed instructions for these tasks, along with the rationale for choosing among various options.

■ Finally, a summary details the tasks performed and also provides a quick list of the major special technical points in the chapter.

# Notational Conventions

The book employs several conventions for presenting special text, figures, and calculations.

## Transact SQL Reserved Words

SQL reserved words such as *float*, *constraint*, or *select* that appear within a sentence are in italics; utilities such as **bcp** and **buildmaster** appear in boldface.

## Transact SQL Code

SQL code chunks appear within grey boxes.

```
declare @maxid int
begin transaction
    update employee set emp_id = 1
    where 1=2
    select @maxid = 1 + max(emp_id)
        from employee
    insert into employee values
    (@maxid,...)
commit transaction
```

## Notes

Notes appear as indented text next to the following icon to emphasize a special instruction or piece of information.

**Note**
A note relates some particularly useful information; pay close attention.

## Warnings

Warnings appear as indented text next to the following icon; they carry much more critical information.

**WARNING!**
A warning cautions or foretells special circumstances which should be noted and/or avoided.

## Figures

Figures appear in double-lined boxes with the title at the top. Any ancillary information to support the figure appears in italicized text below the figure.

Figure 16.1 Primary key delete constraints example------------------------------------

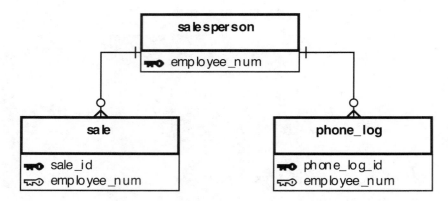

*The salesperson/sale relationship defined above is too critical to allow for cascading deletions of a single salesperson row. Require deletion of all sales information related to a salesperson before allowing the salesperson to be deleted.*

*Salesperson/phone_log does not share the critical nature of the salesperson/sale relationship. There is no apparent reason to restrict deletions based on the existence of phone_log records.*

## *Formulas*

Special formulas for calculating object sizes within the SQL Server are presented to the right of a vertical rule.

### Some Variable-Length Columns

| | |
|---|---|
| 5 | Overhead |
| | Sum of bytes in the fixed-length index keys |
| + ____ | Sum of bytes in the variable-length index keys |
| | Subtotal |
| + | (Subtotal / 256) + 1 |
| + 2 | Overhead |
| | = Clustered-Index Row Size |

# *Before You Begin*

*Physical Database Design is the process of transforming a logical data model into a physical model for a database. Unlike a logical design, a Physical Database Design is optimized for data-access paths, performance requirements, and other constraints of the target environment.*

## Are You Ready?

The fitness and quality of your finished design will depend not only on how you use the techniques outlined herein, but also on how well you did the work that comes before this design stage. Before you can begin the physical design of your database, you must have these things:

- Logical Database Design
  - ★ minimally third normal form
- Transaction characterizations, such as
  - ★ most frequent transactions
  - ★ most complex or resource-intensive transactions
  - ★ transactions which affect the most data
  - ★ distribution of transactions over time
  - ★ mix of *insert*, *update*, *delete*, and *select* statements
  - ★ most critical transactions to the application
- Performance requirements

**Note**

 A detailed list and description of required inputs to physical database design appears in Appendix B of this document. Be sure to go through it carefully to verify that you have everything you need for this process.

# Do You Know? _____

Before you start your Physical Database Design activities, you should know the following information.

## *About physical database design activities*

Physical database design activities are different than other design activities that you may have performed in producing code such as for Cobol, Fortran, or C programs. In those design activities, you concentrate on code control, organization and integration as means to model the required transactions of your system; the system transaction requirements are the basis of your work. Your performance issues typically revolve around CPU utilization, memory swapping and file accesses. You may use flowcharts, dataflow diagrams (DFDs), or pseudocode to express your design. Finally, you tend to maintain a process-oriented view of your system, concentrating on representing the system's transactions.

In contrast, physical database design is a data-oriented activity in which you concentrate on the data that supports the system's transactions. You express your design in the form of entity-relationship diagrams (ERDs). Your performance issues revolve around data accesses, either in cache buffers or through peripheral (disk) I/O. The logical database design, transaction descriptions, and performance requirements are the basis of your work. You perform these design activities to produce data definition language (DDL) statements in SQL (Structured Query Language) code.

Physical database design techniques for a relational database also differ significantly from design techniques you may have used for non-relational databases. In relational database design, you specify tables, columns, relationships among columns, and mechanisms to enforce and maintain the integrity of data. Additionally, physical database design for Sybase SQL Server involves the design of specific structures: databases, tables, columns, rules, defaults, constraints, triggers and other SQL Server structures.

Finally, your physical database design differs from a logical data model in that the physical database design is both optimized and constrained for the target environment—hardware, software, performance requirements, and other constraints. The logical database design focuses on an idealized representation of the data and its interrelationships.

Use the chart in Figure 0.1 as a guide in organizing your physical database design activities. You can perform some activities in parallel or in unison, such as the integrity activities. Some activities, such as defining critical transactions, must be performed in a specific sequence to ensure the greatest effect on the overall physical database design.

Figure 0.1 Physical database design activities ------------------------------------------

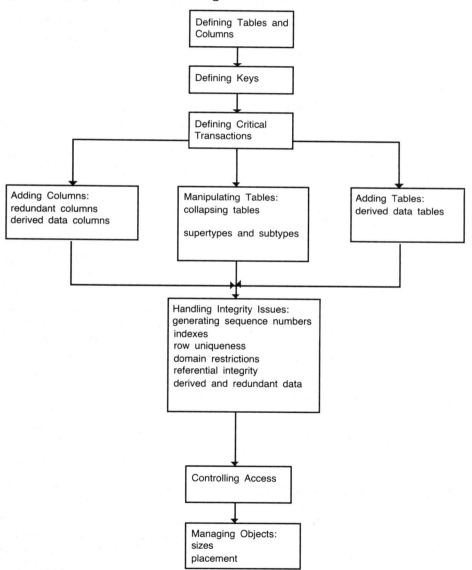

## About physical database design goals

As you read this book and gather techniques for building a good physical database design, you should keep several general goals in mind:

- Embed business rules into the database design.

    When you enforce well-known business rules within your database, through defaults, rules, constraints, stored procedures, or triggers, you encourage universal enforcement of those rules as well as ease of configuration management when changing rules.

- Make it understandable to users.

    A good table design is easier for users (both end-users and applications developers) to use. The names are meaningful and indicative of the data; rows are not filled with many null values; and, while keeping rows from getting too large, they are not so fragmented as to require many joins in order to gather meaningful data.

- Reduce disk I/O.

    Disk I/O is costly compared to memory accesses. Since you are designing your database around a specific hardware and software configuration, optimize for your configuration and for your type of applications. You will see many hints throughout this book to help you in guaranteeing that more of your data resides in RAM so that you do not have to constantly access your data through a disk.

    Similarly, you should evaluate what tools or front-end applications you'll be using to access your database and determine what restrictions your tools may impose on your design. Physical design must always take into account the very real constraints of your system.

- Reduce joins.

    Your logical database design should be optimized, through normalization techniques, to express relationships among data in the truest theoretical manner. In physical database design, you may need to evaluate these relationships and denormalize them to bring the data together more quickly for your specific platform and application needs.

## About database application development

Physical database design, along with the design of your processes and user interfaces, prepares for the development of your applications which will access the data. As you use this book to guide your physical database design activities, keep in mind that your decisions effect the work of the applications development team. To ensure a successful implementation of your design:

1. Consider building several alternate designs, generate a set of sample queries, and monitor performance to determine the best solution to design and performance issues. With large, complex databases, this extra upfront time spent in prototyping and testing can reduce and even eliminate expensive alterations during development and production.

2. Be sure you alert the applications designers and developers as early as possible when you make a change to your physical database design. If data access knowledge is implemented within the database, through views and stored procedures, you'll need to alert the database programmers about the change and its effect on their work.

   As data access knowledge moves out of the database into the front-end applications, you'll also need to alert the applications developers. Such changes can be extremely costly; make alterations judiciously and only after having tested alternatives.

## About denormalization

Denormalization—the process of carefully selecting exceptions to your normalized logical data model—is an important technique in *physical* (though not in *logical*) database design. Denormalization can help you reduce costly join operations, reduce the number of foreign keys requiring maintenance, or quicken data lookups, where the extra code to support denormalization is offset by a matching and required performance gain.

Many of the activities in this book provide denormalization techniques, but they always include advice on when to consider using them, and a note of the offsetting costs associated with each one. You may have to revisit denormalization activities later in the development life cycle, when you can measure the actual behavior of SQL statements.

A normalized logical data model is relatively easy to extend later, as business needs change. However, it is dramtically harder to maintain or change denormalized applications. Excessive or unnecessary denormalization can make later modification difficult or impossible.

**WARNING!**

Denormalize judiciously and with caution. Defer extensive denormalization decisions until detailed performance measurements can be collected and compared with performance requirements.

## *About naming conventions*

Your naming convention must have four qualities: readability, consistency, extensibility, and longevity.

When naming any object, remember that your name has to tell other members of the project team exactly what the object is. This is even more important in the later stages of the system's life cycle.

For object names, use complete words separated by underscores. Avoid all but standard abbreviations, and don't try to keep table names arbitrarily short to save keystrokes. Extra keystrokes are a small price to pay for a data model that is understandable at first glance because it uses names that make sense. If you have names that exceed the SQL Server limit of 30 characters, abbreviate them by removing vowels, and then use your abbreviations consistently.

In UNIX environments, names for database objects and for other system objects use the "_" underscore as a logical separator, and use all lower-case letters. This popular convention produces very readable database object names like "address_table". This convention provides both separation and consistency, and will help you create readable and enduring object names.

A newer naming standard that many system designers like is the object-oriented standard. In this paradigm, "address_table" becomes "addressTable" or "AddressTable". Upper case sets off parts of the object name. Eliminating the underscore increases readability and saves space. The space savings can be significant when a name has four or more parts.

For further guidance in naming SQL Server objects, consult Appendix E: Naming Guidelines.

# Physical Database Design in the Sybase Development Framework and Sybase MethodSet

The Sybase Development Framework (SDF) provides a development methodology within which to perform physical database design. The SDF is a software development process that is intended for use with client/server systems and other computing technologies that are experiencing rapid change. It is based upon a spiral, incremental software development process. The goal of the SDF is to build one complete system or application.

The Sybase MethodSet is a series of publications and tools providing detailed technical guidance to designers and developers. The Methods in the MethodSet focus on Client/Server and Sybase issues. In these Methods, topics are presented as sets of ordered steps, along with the underlying rationale. The Sybase MethodSet is based upon the collective experience of Sybase consultants. Current titles in the Sybase MethodSet include *Physical Database Design for SYBASE SQL Server* and *Naming Guidelines for SYBASE SQL Server*.

Today, many organizations have large investments in existing methodologies. Methods in the Sybase MethodSet can be used with other technical practices in another development methodology. Sybase Development Framework may be populated with other appropriate technical practices. By uncoupling these components, Sybase can provide an "open methodology."

For further information on the SDF and its accompanying Sybase MethodSet, see Appendix A: The Sybase Development Framework and MethodSet.

# Chapter 1
## *Defining Tables and Columns*

## Prologue_____

*In this chapter, you will begin transforming the logical model into a physical model.*

**Must you do this activity? Why or when?**

Yes, for every database, for structural reasons.

**What do you need before you start? How or where do you get it?**
- Normalized logical database design.
- Naming conventions.

**What are the tasks in this activity?**

① Add junction tables where logical design shows entities with many-to-many relationships.

② Assign a name to every table.

③ Assign a name to every column.

④ Specify SQL Server datatypes and lengths for every column.

⑤ Specify other column characteristics.

⑥ Check row sizes.

⑦ Consider maintaining schema integrity.

### *Some things to keep in mind*

■ As you work through later steps, you may need to change some of the names you derive in this step. Plan to review all names later, to ensure that they remain accurate and meaningful.

■ You will assign names to other database objects, such as indexes and triggers. Make all names consistent with the conventions.

■ If your row sizes exceed SQL Server limits, you must reconsider the handling of null values and variable-length datatypes, or the design itself.

# Tasks

*Read through all the tasks in this section before you begin the first task. Perform tasks sequentially, as presented.*

## ① *Adding Junction Tables*

Many-to-many relationships in the logical design are resolved in the physical model through the use of junction or associative tables, as shown in Figure 1.1.

Junction tables have multiple foreign keys which make up the primary key. If the associative table's primary keys are not made up of foreign keys, they are system-generated keys.

Junction tables have one-to-many relationships to the tables they associate. For example, a contractor can have many clients and a client can employ many contractors. Junction tables can break many-to-many relationships into multiple one-to-many relationships.

Figure 1.1 Junction table example ------------------------------------------------------------

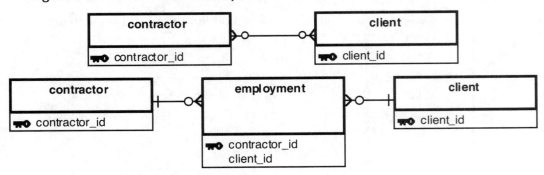

*The employment table is a junction table. It is made up of foreign keys from the contractor and client tables.*

## ② *Assigning a Name to Every Table*

Every table must have a name that is unique within its database. Table names may be up to thirty characters, which gives you room to make them meaningful. Choose names that comply with your chosen naming convention for database objects.

Carry table names forward from their logical entities' names. You may later redefine an entity as multiple tables, or combine multiple entities into one table. In these cases, use common sense to distinguish the new tables while maintaining their correspondence to their entity or entities.

## ③ *Assigning a Name to Every Column*

Every column must have a name that is unique within its table. Column names may be up to thirty characters, which allows them to be meaningful. Choose names that comply with your chosen naming convention for database objects.

Carry column names forward from their logical attributes' names. When creating new columns during the denormalization process, use common sense to name the new columns. Assign identical names to columns that are in primary-key/foreign-key relationships. This documents your intention to use these columns for joins.

## ④ *Specifying a SQL Server Datatype (and Length) for Every Column*

Each column must have a datatype; some datatypes require you to specify a maximum length for the column. In SQL Server 10.x, all system datatype names are case-insensitive. The choice of datatype and length determines the type of data and range of values the column will hold.

When choosing a datatype, you must carefully consider the potential range of values that will be stored in the column. A common mistake is to underestimate the size required, and fail to allow for future changes in business requirements. You need a datatype large enough to allow for future changes and small enough to avoid wasting space.

Table 1.1 describes the datatypes available in the SYBASE SQL Server. The datatypes are further described following the table.

Here are some further considerations about each of the datatypes shown in the table.

### Exact numeric datatypes

Exact numeric datatypes (*int, smallint, tinyint, numeric, decimal*) have two main properties. First, they typically store a value in less space than a character type would take. Second, they automatically exclude nonnumeric values. In addition, *tinyint, smallint,* and *int* preserve their accuracy during arithmetic operations.

3

## Table 1.1 Datatype Ranges and Storage Sizes----------------------------------------

| Datatype | Holds | Range | Bytes of Storage |
|---|---|---|---|
| EXACT NUMERIC DATATYPES | | | |
| *tinyint* | whole numbers | 0 to 255 | 1 |
| *smallint* | whole numbers | $2^{15}$-1 to -$2^{15}$ | 2 |
| *int* | whole numbers | $2^{31}$-1 to -$2^{31}$ | 4 |
| *numeric(p,s)* | decimal point numbers | $10^{38}$-1 to -$10^{38}$ | 2 to 17 |
| *decimal(p,s)* | decimal point numbers | $10^{38}$-1 to -$10^{38}$ | 2 to 17 |
| APPROXIMATE NUMERIC DATATYPES | | | |
| *float(p)* | floating point numbers | machine dependent | 4 or 8 |
| *double precision* | floating point numbers | machine dependent | 8 |
| *real* | floating point numbers | machine dependent | 4 |
| MONEY DATATYPES | | | |
| *money* | money | (see note below) | 8 |
| *smallmoney* | money | 214,748.3647 to -214,748.3648 | 4 |
| DATE AND TIME DATATYPES | | | |
| *datetime* | date and time | January 1, 1753 to December 31, 9999 | 8 |
| *smalldatetime* | date and time | January 1, 1900 to June 6, 2079 | 4 |
| CHARACTER DATATYPES | | | |
| *char(n)* | fixed-length character | 255 characters or less | n |
| *varchar(n)* | character varying, char varying | 255 characters or less | actual entry length |

Table 1.1 (continued) ---------------------------------------------------------------------------

| Datatype | Holds | Range | Bytes of Storage |
|----------|-------|-------|------------------|
| *nchar(n)* | national character, national char | 255 characters or less | n * @@ncharsize |
| *nvarchar(n)* | nchar varying, national char varying, national character varying | 255 characters or less | @@ncharsize * number of characters |
| **BINARY DATATYPES** | | | |
| *text(n)* | character | $2^{31}$-1 characters or less | Minimum 2K in multiples of 2K bytes + 16 bytes for address. |
| *bit* | bit | 0 or 1 | 8 per byte |
| *binary(n)* | fixed-length binary | 255 bytes or less | n |
| *varbinary(n)* | variable-length binary | 255 bytes or less | up to n |
| *image* | binary | $2^{31}$-1 bytes or less | Minimum 2K in multiples of 2K bytes + 16 bytes for address. |

- *The range for the money datatype is 922,337,203,685,477.5807 to −922,337,203,685,477.5808.*
- *For char, varchar, nchar, and nvarchar, the default length is 1.*
- *Support for null adds 1 byte of overhead.*

SQL Server 10.x provides two other exact numeric types, *numeric* and *decimal*, for numbers that include decimal points. Data stored in columns of these datatypes is packed to conserve disk space. Additionally, the datatypes preserve accuracy to the least significant digit after arithmetic operations. Only the *numeric* datatype with a scale of 0 can be used for the automatically generated sequence number, the IDENTITY column, provided as an option in SQL Server 10.x.

Use the *int* numeric type as much as possible when choosing numeric datatypes for join operations. The 4-byte *int* can be much faster than other numeric types in a join due to its compatibility with the native instruction set.

Numeric datatypes are compact, but do potentially incur considerable application overhead because they force the application to perform print and string conversions. See "Storing numeric strings with character datatypes" for alternatives. Furthermore, when defining numeric columns, keep in mind that these datatypes ignore leading zeros, and you may need leading zeroes for columns such as social security numbers (SSN). For example, avoid defining an SSN column as an *int*, since you would have to make the application replace the suppressed leading zeros.

Because numeric types do not allow nonnumeric characters, numeric strings, such as SSNs, cannot be stored with embedded dashes or slashes. The application has to format the data every time it is displayed.

## Approximate numeric datatypes

Approximate numeric datatypes (float, double precision, real) can tolerate rounding during arithmetic operations. The approximate numeric types are especially suited to data that covers a wide range of values.

## Money datatypes

Use *money* and *smallmoney* for decimal currency entries: *smallmoney* is a space-saving alternative to the standard *money* datatype. These two datatypes extend a useful set of printing and consistency functions to your monetary data since they maintain the two decimal place rounding of all data values and allow you to precede input with a U.S. dollar sign ($). For greater accuracy in your calculations, however, consider using *numeric or decimal* datatypes instead. The trade-off lies in calculation time versus printing conversion time.

You can use *money* and *smallmoney* to store monetary values other than U.S. dollars, but be prepared to handle all conversion operations in your application.

If your application requires precision greater than two decimal places for money transactions, you will have to use the *float* datatype and use application-level printing functions to show the values as monetary.

## Date and time datatypes

Use the *datetime* and *smalldatetime* datatypes for storing dates and times of day: *smalldatetime* simply provides date values in half the data space (only four bytes) but only provides accuracy to the minute versus to 3.33 milliseconds. You can input values three different ways and SQL Server handles printing and comparison functions for you. You can even do some arithmetic functions on *datetime* values using the built-in date functions.

## Character datatypes

SQL Server supports three ways to store character data: *char*, *varchar*, and *text*. The *text* datatype is addressed in a later section.

The *char* datatype is used for fixed-length character data; the length specified is the actual amount of storage used. Because of its performance edge over the variable character datatype, *varchar*, use *char* when the length of the character data is predictable and/or small.

**WARNING!**

If you specify *null* for a *char* datatype, SQL Server then treats the column/variable as a *varchar*. This may cause conversion delays when joining with a true *char* column/variable and may prevent the Server from using that column at all for optimization.

The *varchar* datatype is for variable-length data; the length specified is the maximum the column will hold. This datatype adds one byte to track the data length, but then uses only what is actually needed. Use this datatype for larger columns (rule of thumb: longer than five characters) for which the data length will vary, such as addresses.

The five-character minimum for a *varchar* column is an approximate break-even point. If the length of the character value will be no more than five, it makes sense to declare the column to be *char(5)* and avoid the overhead associated with *varchar* columns.

## Binary datatypes

SQL Server supports four ways to store binary data: *bit*, *binary* (and *varbinary*), *image*, and *timestamp*. The *image* type is addressed in a later section.

The *bit* datatype stores a single Boolean value, usually referenced as 0 or 1. It is useful for flags in that it has an implicit rule associated with it. *Bit* is less useful if it must be converted for user presentation such as a "Y" or "N" value. However, it provides the binary values of "Y" and "N" without necessarily taking up the same amount of space for each value.

Storage size is 1 bit. Multiple *bit* columns in the same table can be collected into one or more bytes. For example, seven *bit* columns fit into one byte; nine *bit* columns take two bytes; and one *bit* column in a table takes one byte. Therefore, you can realize sizing benefits only if you use more than one of these datatypes per table.

The *binary* and *varbinary* datatypes are the complements of *char* and *varchar*. The same issues apply. The difference is that the data stored is referenced as bits instead of ASCII characters. A typical use of these types is storing bit masks.

SQL Server provides a user-defined datatype, *timestamp*, defined as *varbinary(8)* NULL. *timestamp* does not provide a date value; rather, it holds a sequence number associated with a given access. Use this valuable datatype to police accesses and potential changes to tables in a high-volume multi-user environment. A column of datatype *timestamp* and with the name "timestamp" is mandatory in tables that are to be browsed in Client Library applications. Furthermore, it is automatically added to the table definition of any table containing a *text* or *image* datatype column.

Each time a row from a table with a *timestamp* is accessed, the current sequence value is returned with the row. If the row is updated in any way, compare the subsequent timestamp against the current timestamp to determine if the update request can be allowed. The system function *tsequal* compares timestamp values to prevent an update on a row that has been modified since it was selected for browsing. Use it in order to avoid lost updates.

Consult the SQL Server Reference Manual, Volume 1, "Datatypes" discussion for details about how to define this special datatype.

## Text and image datatypes

The *text* and *image* datatypes are used to store large volumes of character data or binary data. *char* and *binary* datatypes cannot exceed 255 bytes per column; *text* and *image* data is a linked list of pages, limited only by the amount of available space up to two gigabytes per record. Binary data stored in this way are sometimes referred to as "blobs," or *b*inary, *l*arge *ob*jects.

Possible uses of the *text* datatype include:

- comments
- small or large documents

For each *text* column defined and initialized in a row, at least one data page of 2048 bytes is reserved for that column's use, regardless of how large the *text* data actually is. If the average size of the comment field does not exceed 255 bytes, but you need to support larger comments, use multiple *char* or *varchar* columns for the field versus one *text* column. A table comprised only of these fields accompanied by a unique row identifier from the parent table can support such a scheme and use far fewer data pages than *text* fields would.

Possible uses of the *image* datatype include:

- maps
- photographs
- blueprints and mechanical drawings

## User-defined datatypes

SQL Server user-defined datatypes may be used to represent the SQL Server-provided datatype, length, and null status, providing consistency among columns that are repeated in different tables.

The real power of user-defined datatypes is they let you enforce domain restrictions by binding rules and defaults to the datatypes, rather than to the individual columns. Similarly, using a user-defined datatype on both a primary key and a foreign key guarantees type compatibility in joining their respective tables. This too can help to reduce errors.

## Storing numeric strings with character datatypes

You might store a numeric string such as a social security number (SSN) as an *int* (four bytes), *char(9)* (nine bytes), or *char(11)* (eleven bytes). *Varchar* would not be appropriate because the length of the data is consistent. Defining the column as an *int* uses less space but incurs the application overhead discussed under numeric datatypes.

Suppose you define a SSN as a *char(9)*. Because character datatypes do not suppress leading zeros, they can handle an SSN like this one:

012345678

If you define a SSN as a *char(11)*, you can store it with the embedded formatting characters, as follows:

012-34-5678

Make your choice between numeric versus character datatypes based on the primary functions of your application. If you must perform many more arithmetic calculations than printing, numeric datatypes are the best choice. A print-intensive application, on the other hand, can benefit greatly from *char* representation of the numbers.

## Join considerations in specifying datatypes

Wherever possible, columns that you use to join tables should be specified with *exactly the same datatype*. For example, a join between *char* and *varchar* columns, while syntactically acceptable, will result in an implicit and costly datatype conversion. Moreover, if the datatypes are not exactly the same, the optimizer may not choose the index you intend it to use, based on its estimation of conversion time.

9

# ⑤ *Specifying Other Column Characteristics*

With SQL Servers prior to release 10.x, you can only specify the datatype and nullability characteristics for a column. As of release 10.x, you can also specify default, identity, reference, and constraint characteristics within the column definition.

## Null

A null value represents an unknown value or a case where a column will not have a value because of context. As you create tables, define each column to allow or prohibit null values. When creating tables, the default SQL Server is not to allow nulls, though the ANSI standard default allows nulls. Be aware of the default for your particular configuration.

Consider these reasons for allowing or prohibiting *nulls* in column definitions.

### Reasons to allow nulls

- *Null values are meaningful!* Blanks and zeros are not nulls; a null means "unknown" or "not applicable."
- The column's value will not be available when the row is created.
- The column's value will not be provided for some rows (context sensitive).
- The column is part of a foreign key and the referential integrity strategy for the database specifies setting foreign keys to *null* when they are "orphans."
- When converting legacy systems, values of asterisks, blanks, all nines or zeros are often indications that the column should allow nulls.

### Reasons to prohibit nulls

- Nulls are not unique. Do not use nullable columns for primary keys, because null values are treated as duplicates. However, this situation is rare and more an indicator of incorrect key selection than a problem with nulls.
- In all cases, SQL Server treats nullable columns as variable-length columns. This has negative performance implications of approximately 30% versus an identical column which does not allow nulls.
- Null values affect calculations. Mathematical operations return null if any value involved is null; an unknown operand must yield an unknown result. Some aggregate functions—such as *count()* and *avg()*—ignore null values. You can avoid these behaviors by dynami-

cally substituting values for nulls, with the *isnull()* function, but you should consider a default value instead of allowing nulls.

- Comparisons which involve null values result in UNKNOWN results, even when being compared to other null values. As a result, columns which may be used for joins are bad candidates for allowing nulls. In order to join based on null values, use the *isnull()* function to replace the nulls with some other value. Three special comparisons involving nulls will return TRUE when *expression* is any column, variable or literal or combination of these, which evaluates as *null*:

  1. *expression* **is [not] null**
  2. *expression* = NULL and *expression* != NULL
  3. *expression* = @x and *expression* != @x, where @x is a variable or parameter containing NULL. This exception facilitates writing stored procedures with null default parameters.

## Default

The *default* characteristic specifies a default value for a column and can be a constant expression: *user* to insert the name of the user who is performing the insert, or *null* to insert the null value. You can use this in place of the *create default/ sp_bindefault* syntax. *default* provides domain integrity, as described in Chapter 15, "Handling Domain Integrity."

## Identity

You can specify one column in your table as having the *identity* property. The column stores sequential numbers that are generated automatically by SQL Server. You can find more information about this property in Chapter 12, "Generating Sequence Numbers."

## Constraint

A column may also have one or more constraint properties associated with it. Some of the constraints (*unique*, *primary key*, and *foreign key...references*) take names. Specify names that conform to your naming standards and which clearly associate the constraint with the table and column. The *check* constraint does not take a name.

### Key Constraints

With SQL Server 10.x, you can now specify *unique*, *primary key*, and *foreign key...references* with the column definition. For example, the *unique* referential integrity constraint can be used in place of the *create unique index* syntax. For

11

more information about enforcing referential integrity using these techniques, consult Chapter 16, "Handling Referential Integrity."

### Check

The *check* constraint allows you to specify a rule condition associated within the column definition versus the pre-SQL Server 10.x *create rule/sp_bindrule* syntax. *check* provides domain integrity as described in Chapter 15, "Handling Domain Restrictions."

# ⑥ *Checking the Row Size*

With a clear understanding of good naming standards and an overview of the available datatype definitions well in hand, you may feel fully prepared to start defining your tables and their associated columns. But you have one more very fundamental puzzle piece to consider before you begin your definition wizardry—the row size. In defining your table columns, you must consider SQL Server's page and row accounting overhead. Here are the main concerns:

- No one row may exceed the available space on one standard data page.
- The standard data page size is 2048 bytes (4096 on Stratus computers), minus SQL Server overhead bytes.
- Every row instance on a page adds at least one byte of overhead to the page's accounting bytes.
- Any column defined as either null or variable-length adds one byte of overhead to the row's accounting bytes.
- Any variable-length column whose offset from the starting address of the row exceeds 256 or a multiple of 256 adds at least one byte of overhead to the row's accounting bytes.

## Page-accounting constraints on row size

A data page within SQL Server consists of 2048 bytes (except Stratus systems, which support twice that amount). SQL Server divides the page into two primary sections:

- Server Accounting Section

  SQL Server requires overhead bytes to acquaint itself with the general profile of rows on the page. This accounting information also supports SQL Server's view of the page in terms of the table and database that populate the page.

- Data Rows

  Every row on the page resides in one contiguous set of space, where each row takes up space for the column data and for row details such as:

  ★ a row number (not user accessible)—one byte

  ★ the number of variable-length and null columns in the row—one byte

The largest space available for data rows is then 2048 minus the minimal number of SQL Server accounting bytes needed to maintain the page. This turns out to be 2015 bytes. Thus, the largest possible row is theoretically 2015.

In truth, the *largest possible row size is 1962* , when you factor in considerations for both the row accounting overhead and log page accounting limitations.

If you have a need to maintain data which exceeds this 1962-byte limit, consider using text or image data types in which to store your data. Either of these data types simply adds its 16-byte address to the row size. But be forewarned! If you do not allow nulls for such columns, you automatically reserve a 2048-byte page for your column's use, whether or not you tried to store data in the column. This becomes a crucial consideration when calculating overall database size.

Another solution to the 1962-byte limit is to split your table into two tables and then join them as necessary. (See Chapter 7, "Splitting Tables," for more information on this technique.) However, even after you have split the table, you cannot obtain more than 1962 bytes in any one row of a query's result set.

## Row-accounting constraints on row size

SQL Server stores more than data within a data row. It also conceals useful information about the row within the data elements of the row. For this reason, row accounting may add to your row-size considerations. In fact, you may be able to significantly alter the size of your rows—and how efficiently they are stored on the data page—by judiciously applying your knowledge of datatype accounting overheads as you define table columns.

Each row instance has a 2-byte overhead, used to identify the row and to signal whether or not the row contains variable-length data. Additional overhead is incurred for variable or null column definitions as follows:

- The first variable-length or null column defined adds a 5-byte overhead to the row.

- Each additional variable-length or null column adds at least 1 byte of accounting overhead. If a column is the first column to start at an offset greater than 256 bytes from the start of the row, it adds 1 byte of accounting information to aid in tracking the starting address of subsequent data columns in the row. (A byte is also added for each new column which starts at 512, or any other multiple of 256, bytes from the row's starting address.)

In essence, the row-accounting information increases in size as the row's variable-length and nullable columns increase in size. The row-specific accounting information indicates location and size of nonfixed columns. (Fixed-column offsets and sizes are derived in the *syscolumns* rows for the table.) It also tracks the offset from the beginning of the row to the end of the variable-length column data.

Additionally, the row-accounting information grows according to the size of the row. Calculate the specific number of extra accounting bytes by dividing the total row size by 256 and adding one.

For a detailed algorithm to calculate table, index, text page, image page, and transaction log sizes, consult Chapter 20, "Managing Object Sizes."

## ⑦ *Providing Schema Integrity*

SQL Server 10.x provides a mechanism for enforcing integrity at the database schema level. Subsequent chapters of this book present mechanisms for providing data, domain, and referential integrity in your physical design.

You can use the *create schema* syntax to additionally provide schema integrity. This SQL construct creates a new collection of tables, views, and permissions for a database user as if all enclosed create statements and grant/revoke statements were one transaction, thus ensuring the integrity of the created objects with respect to one another and with respect to users' access to them.

# Epilogue

*The following list summarizes the tasks performed as you began to transform the logical model into a physical model.*

❶ Added junction tables where logical design shows entities with many-to-many relationships.

❷ Assigned a name to every table.

❸ Assigned a name to every column.

❹ Specified SQL Server datatypes and lengths for every column.

❺ Specified other column characteristics.

❻ Checked row sizes.
❼ Considered maintaining schema integrity.

## *Some things to remember:*

▶ Set up a naming convention and stick to it.

▶ When you need a numeric datatype to participate in a join, consider using the *int* numeric type as it can speed up the join operation compared with other numeric datatypes.

▶ If you specify null for a fixed datatype, SQL Server treats it as a variable datatype thereafter.

▶ For each *text* column defined in a row, at least one data page of 2048 bytes is reserved for that column, regardless of how large the *text* data actually is.

▶ Consider using the SQL Server 10.x *default*, *identity*, and *key* constraint features to enforce additional integrity in your data definitions.

▶ Allowing nulls for a column has negative performance implications of approximately 30% versus an identical column which does not allow nulls.

▶ A single row cannot exceed 1962 bytes.

▶ A row cannot cross a page boundary.

▶ A single data page has 2016 bytes available for data rows and their accompanying accounting bytes.

# Chapter 2
## *Defining Keys*

## Prologue

*In this chapter, you will define*

- *the primary key, a column (or set of columns) that uniquely identifies each row of a table in the physical model, and*

- *foreign key(s), a column or columns that refer to the primary key of another table.*

**Must you do this activity? Why or when?**

Yes; it is always required, for structural reasons.

**What do you need before you start? How or where do you get it?**

- Table and column definitions.
- Normalized logical database design.

**What are the tasks in this activity?**

① Assess logical keys by compiling a list of candidate primary keys from your logical design.

② Specify the best primary key, if there is more than one choice.

③ Specify foreign keys.

④ Consider using surrogate keys. If any primary keys were made into surrogates, find all the affected foreign keys.

### *Some things to keep in mind*

■ Plan to revisit this activity after performing any denormalization activity.

17

# Tasks_____

*Read through all the tasks in this section before you begin the first task. Perform tasks sequentially, as presented.*

## ① *Assessing Logical Keys*

The logical design, preferably represented by an entity relationship diagram, should specify logical primary and foreign keys for the entities. Use these as a starting point for specifying keys for the tables.

## ② *Specifying Primary Keys*

Consider the following criteria when selecting a column (or set of columns) as each table's primary key:

- There is always only one primary key for a table. (Implementors should use the *sp_primarykey* stored procedure to document the key selection in the actual database.)
- The primary key must uniquely identify the row.

If faced with more than one candidate primary key:

- Select the one which transactions will know about most often. This will avoid additional lookups.
- Select the shortest one when used in indexes (if all other considerations appear equal.)
- Consider what other keys are available in other tables on which to join.

If you choose to use the SQL Server 10.x *primary key* constraint within the *create table* syntax, SQL Server constrains the values of the indicated column or columns so that no two rows can have the same value, and so that the value cannot be null. Additionally, the constraint creates a unique index that can only be dropped if the constraint is dropped using *alter table*.

## ③ *Specifying Foreign Keys*

Control foreign key placement by the relationship type.

*One-to-many Relationships*

- In one-to-many relationships, foreign keys reside on the "many" side of the relationship. See Figure 2.1 for an example.

## Figure 2.1 One-to-many relationship example ------------------------------------

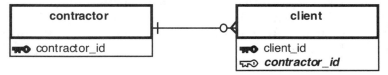

*The contractor_id in the client table is a foreign key.*

### *One-to-one Relationships*

- In one-to-one relationships, place the foreign key in the table with fewer rows. The smaller table is usually easy to determine.

Consider the example of a portion of a state's motor vehicles database, shown in Figure 2.2.

## Figure 2.2 One-to-one relationship example -----------------------------------------

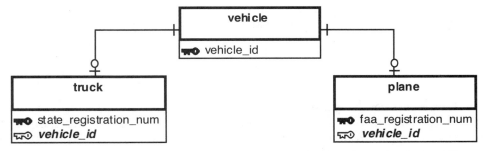

*Because there are fewer trucks than vehicles and fewer planes than vehicles, vehicle_id becomes a foreign key in the truck and plane tables.*

If you choose to use the SQL Server 10.x *foreign key* constraint within the *create table* syntax, SQL Server specifies that the listed column(s) are foreign keys in the table, whose target keys are the columns (*ref_column(s)*) in the table (*ref_table*) listed in the following *references* clause. The columns in the referenced table must be constrained by a unique index.

## ④ *Using Surrogate Keys*

Surrogate keys (also referred to as contrived or artificial keys) are columns with no business meaning that are added to tables to represent one or more existing columns. Surrogate-key candidates include:

- tables with very large or multi-column primary keys
- text columns that require indexing

**19**

A surrogate key does not replace the logical primary key; instead it redefines the primary key for use as a foreign key in other tables. As an example, consider the titles table, shown in Figure 2.3, from the sample database—pubs (a full schema is located in Appendix B). The title_id column of the titles table is a surrogate-key value and replaces the title, pubname, and pub_date fields as the primary key.

Figure 2.3 Surrogate-key example ----------------------------------------------------------

| titles |
| --- |
| *title_id* |
| title |
| type |
| pub_id |
| price |
| advance |
| total_sales |
| notes |
| pubdate |
| contract |

Large keys can have a significant effect on overall system performance. An increase of one or two I/Os per data access may not seem like much for an individual data access, but if that data is accessed several thousand times per transaction, the impact is significant.

On occasion, you may need to have the key values made up of multiple columns. If data can be uniquely identified only by means of a large combined key, you can invent a new, surrogate key, to replace the large key value. For instance, a smaller key value, such as an employee_id, uniquely identifies an employee, just as the set of last_name, first_name, and middle_initial is a unique identifier. The surrogate key means nothing to the particular entity being identified, but does serve as an internal means of identification of the data.

The surrogate key contributes to better performance by representing a smaller value than the real values that identify the data. The smaller key occupies less space in the index. Therefore the entire index is smaller, and subsequently faster to access and scan.

When used as a foreign key, the smaller surrogate key will:

- Make it easier to write SQL code to join tables, primarily when the surrogate key redefines a multi-column primary key.

- Decrease the size of the table, because a much smaller surrogate key replaces the long or multi-part foreign key. The smaller row size allows more data rows to fit on a data page.

- Decrease the size of foreign-key indexes. The smaller key size lets more index rows fit on a page, giving you a B-Tree with a smaller height and fewer pages for storage.

- Increase performance on queries accessing the tables with the surrogate key values, since more rows can be read in one I/O operation. Both the smaller foreign-key index size and the smaller table improve the processing rate.

- Simplify some cascading update issues.

The introduction of surrogate keys will increase the row size of the table containing the primary surrogate key value. This will result in a larger table size, with fewer rows per page. Also, surrogate keys may require enforcement of unique values on both the surrogate key and the underlying multiple-column values, which means you may need multiple indexes on the table rather than just one.

Carefully document all surrogate-key instances and their expected use.

Generating surrogate keys typically involves generating a unique, sequential integer, discussed in Chapter 12, "Generating Sequence Numbers." You must weigh the overhead associated with generating a unique, surrogate key against the performance benefits. Additionally, with SQL Server 10.x, you may choose to use the *identity* column as the surrogate-key to uniquely identify a row. Consult the SQL Server Reference Manual, Volume 1, for further information about *identity*.

# Epilogue

*The following list summarizes the tasks performed as you defined primary keys and foreign keys.*

❶ Assessed logical keys by compiling a list of candidate primary keys from your logical design.

❷ Specified the best primary key, if there is more than one choice.

❸ Specified foreign keys.

❹ Considered using surrogate keys. If any primary keys were made into surrogates, found all the affected foreign keys.

## *Some things to remember:*

▶ The SQL Server 10.x *primary key* constraint creates a unique index that can only be dropped if the constraint is dropped using *alter table*.

▶ Using a surrogate key for the foreign key value in a row not only reduces the data row size; it also reduces the total number of pages in any accompanying nonclustered index.

# Chapter 3
## *Identifying Critical Transactions*

## Prologue_____

*In this chapter, you will identify business transactions that are:*

- *high-value*
- *mission-critical*
- *frequently performed*
- *costly in terms of I/O and CPU time*

**Must you do this activity? Why or when?**

Yes, required for best performance.

**What do you need before you start? How or where do you get it?**

- Transaction specifications from logical design.
- Logical-process design of the application.
- Gross object-size estimates.

**What are the tasks in this activity?**

① Identify important transactions.

② Identify transactions that are not likely to meet performance requirements.

## *Some things to keep in mind*

■  This list of critical transactions will become the basis for performance-related considerations in later activities.

# Tasks

*Read through all the tasks in this section before you begin the first task. Perform tasks sequentially, as presented.*

## ① *Identifying Important Transactions*

To determine the physical database design, you must understand the transactions the system must deal with: how will the data be accessed? You must also understand the performance requirements of the system.

To understand the transactions and performance requirements, you need to know:

- types of transactions (*select*, *insert*, *update*, *delete*)
- tables and columns affected by each transaction
- selection criteria
- whether selection criteria are fixed or variable (i.e., pre-defined queries or ad hoc queries)
- frequency and volume of each transaction
- how many rows (percent) are typically affected (selected or modified) by each transaction
- size (number of rows) of tables involved in transactions
- for tables with a one-to-many relationship, what are the smallest, largest, and average numbers of rows in the "many" table associated with a row in the "one" table (i.e., the average invoice record 3 line items, at least 1 line item, and at most 30 line items)
- what existing reports rely upon which transactions
- when the transaction is executed—during the day or after hours
- relative importance of each transaction—who uses it, how often, how critical is it to the business process
- response time or throughput desired for a given transaction
- general response-time requirements—for example, whether quick retrievals are more important than fast updates and inserts
- security and integrity provisions: these checks must be considered as part of the transactions
- audit requirements—what transactions must be tracked, what information about the transaction must be tracked

- how many tables will be joined
- sort order

## ② *Identifying Transactions Unlikely to Meet Performance Requirements*

Your physical database design must provide for the best performance of the most important transactions. These critical transactions usually are:

- most frequently performed transactions
- transactions performed by key personnel
- transactions affecting many rows
- transactions affecting many tables
- resource-intensive transactions
- mission-critical transactions
- high-value transactions

Also, attention must be paid to distribution of transactions with respect to time, if this is not uniform (for example, peak periods and specific run times).

# Epilogue

*The following list summarizes the tasks performed as you identified critical transactions.*

❶ Identified important transactions.
❷ Identified transactions that are not likely to meet performance requirements.

# Chapter 4
## *Adding Redundant Columns*

## Prologue_____

*In this chapter, you will add column(s) to a table, duplicate column(s) that exist in other table(s).*

> **Must you do this activity? Why or when?**
>
> Yes, required when an unacceptable number of joins is needed to perform a critical transaction.
>
> **What do you need before you start? How or where do you get it?**
>
> - List of critical transactions derived from Chapter 3.
> - Table and column definitions.
> - Naming conventions.
>
> **What are the tasks in this activity?**
>
> ① Identify the join paths of the critical transactions.
> ② Count the joins of the critical transactions.
> ③ Add redundant columns as needed.

### *Some things to keep in mind*

■ Redundant columns may result in data integrity problems. To prevent these, you must keep track of any added redundant columns, and specify mechanisms to maintain their integrity when you get to Chapter 17.

■ Performance testing may also reveal the need to add redundant columns.

# Tasks

*You may want to add redundant columns to a table in order to reduce the number of joins required by critical transactions. The following tasks define techniques for doing so.*

Read through all the tasks in this section before you begin the first task. Perform tasks sequentially, as presented.

## ① *Identifying Transactions*

If you anticipate performance problems with critical SQL statements that join to retrieve columns for the purpose of selection or filtering, then the tables used by the join operation may be candidates for denormalization. You can attempt to identify such situations during physical design by conducting performance testing on the tables and functions in question. Avoid guessing about performance; use your test results to help guide your denormalization activities.

## ② *Determining the Number of Joins*

Examine all the critical transactions' use of your database's tables, adding up the number of joins in which each table is participant.

Consider the sample database, pubs (located in Appendix B). If a critical query extracts information from the titles table and joins with the publishers table to obtain the publisher's name, and does it too slowly, consider adding the pubname columns from the publishers table to the titles table. This eliminates a costly join.

## ③ *Copying One or More Redundant Columns*

Now is the time to add redundant columns in order to reduce the number of joins. In this approach, an exact copy of the columns referenced by the join are copied into the outer table from the inner table, as shown in Figure 4.1.

You provide better performance to the critical query if you eliminate the join with the publishers table. However, you also add overhead to maintain the replicated publisher name column in the titles table. You must decide whether the gain in performance is worth the cost in overhead. If the redundant column is fairly volatile (subject to frequent modifications), you may opt against redundancy as a solution.

## Figure 4.1 Redundant column example ------------------------------------------------

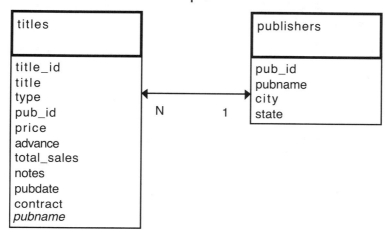

*In this example, pubname has been added to the titles table. Often, it is helpful to have a naming convention that can identify a column as redundant ( e.g. pubname_t).*

Column-level denormalization on lookup or parent tables provides the following benefits:

- Better response times or throughput through the elimination of the join.
- The chance to eliminate a foreign key, primarily if you can collapse the lookup table.
- The reduction of lock contention; this cuts down blocking or deadlock situations depending on the nature of the transactions.

You should be aware that:

- The modified table will grow in size. Adding column(s) to the table will result in a wider row. In particular, fewer rows can be stored on a data page; therefore, storing the table-level information takes more pages.
- The larger number of data pages will slow performance of queries not benefiting from the elimination of the join, as the number of I/Os required to process the table is greater.
- The duplicated column data will require maintenance, perhaps through triggers, to ensure that duplicated columns are kept up to date. This performance penalty can be severe in situations where the column to be duplicated is volatile.

Balance these trade-offs against using redundant columns to reduce joins.

# Epilogue

*The following list summarizes the tasks performed as you added column(s) to a table and duplicated column(s) that existed in other table(s).*

❶ Identified the join paths of the critical transactions.

❷ Counted the joins of the critical transactions.

❸ Added redundant columns to reduce the number of joins required by the critical transactions.

## *Some things to remember:*

▶ Adding a redundant column will increase the table's size, allowing fewer rows per data page. Recalculate your table size accordingly.

▶ The duplicated column will require integrity maintenance such as a trigger which could cause a performance penalty, particularly when the column to be duplicated is highly volatile.

# Chapter 5
## *Adding Derived Columns*

## Prologue_____

*In this chapter, you will add derived columns to tables, based on the values of, or existence of values in, other columns in other tables.*

**Must you do this activity? Why or when?**

Yes, when you expect that the performance requirements for a critical transaction will not be met because of a costly, recurring calculation based on relatively static data, and when the derived columns you are considering fit into an existing table.

This step is generally suitable if the data under the calculation changes much less often than the application needs to use it.

**What do you need before you start? How or where do you get it?**

• List of critical transactions from Chapter 3.

• Table and column definitions.

• Naming conventions.

**What are the tasks in this activity?**

① Identify critical database transactions that rely on recurring calculations for which the underlying data does not change often.

② Add derived columns to suitable tables.

③ Consider adding columns for use as indexes for text data.

### *Some things to keep in mind*

■ Derived columns may result in data integrity problems. To prevent these, you must keep track of any added derived columns and specify mechanisms to maintain their integrity when you get to Chapter 17.

■ Performance testing may also reveal the need to add derived columns.

■ If you discover you need an entire table of derived columns, consult Chapter 10, Adding Tables for Derived Data.

# Tasks

*Read through all the tasks in this section before you begin the first task. Perform tasks sequentially, as presented.*

## ① *Identifying Transactions*

Adding derived data is most useful for queries that require access to the derived columns for selecting or filtering, and have no other requirement to join with the detail table. Reports or decision-support queries typically benefit from this denormalization.

**Note**
If you discover that your derived data is updated more often than it is read, you may choose to simply maintain the data through a view which incorporates the calculation into the result set. Choose derived columns to store derived information when your data is queried more often than modified.

## ② *Considering Derived Columns and Intra-row Derived Data*

Typically the derived data is aggregate or calculated data based on groups of data stored in detail records of another table.

Derived data may include:

• Column data aggregated with SQL Server aggregate functions such as *sum()* or *avg()* over N detail rows.

• Column data which is calculated using formulas over N rows. Complex calculations of this nature may be performed by Open Server Applications.

• Counts of detail rows matching specific criteria.

For example, in the pubs sample database, the titles table contains one derived column value, total_sales. This column sums up all the sales for the given title_id. In Figure 5.1, the total_sales column is derived from the salesdetail table, and is maintained through *insert*, *update*, and *delete* triggers on the sales-detail table.

This technique improves response times and throughput by means of:

- reduced I/O, formerly needed to perform the join operation with the detail table
- reduced demand on CPU to perform the join and necessary calculations

**Figure 5.1 Derived data column example**------------------------------------------------

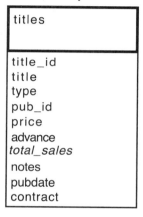

You should be aware that:

- the parent table will grow in size, to accommodate the columns added to hold derived data;
- the SQL operations that do not benefit from this denormalization may run slower, as more pages must be processed within multiple-row operations;
- the detail tables will require triggers to maintain the derived data in the parent tables. This can be costly if the column to be computed is volatile.

If you expect performance problems when computing values derived from columns within the same row, then consider storing the precomputed value within the row.

**Note**

This technique is most beneficial where the columns used for the calculations are not volatile.

For example, if the sales table includes the price column to capture the price of a title at time of ordering, then you can add an intra-row derived column, total, to contain the total price of the item order. (See Figure 5.2.)

**Figure 5.2 Intra-row derived data column example** ------------------------------------

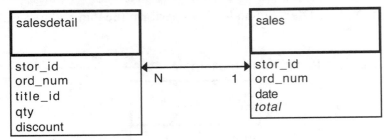

*When item-level information is added to an order in the orders table, the price of the book and the quantity ordered are extended out to the new column total to contain the total for the item line.*

The precomputation eliminates the need to perform calculations on the fly. This technique saves CPU resources, and is quite attractive when the formula for the calculation is complicated.

The technique also lends itself well to compute-server installations, where a project team plans to use Open Server-based compute servers. In this instance, intense calculations are performed by Open Server applications, which run on computers designed to perform calculations. The intra-row derived data is derived upon row insert, or upon updates to columns that make up the computed column.

## ③ *Considering Adding Columns to Index Text Columns*

If your text data will not fit into a SQL Server *varchar* datatype, which at most can contain 255 characters, then the SQL Server *text* datatype may be considered. SQL Server cannot index *text* fields, thus SQL operations that do keyword searches using the *like* function will scan all pages for the *text* column. This operation is costly, particularly when the *text* information is large.

One method to improve performance is to add an abstract key that fits into the SQL Server *varchar* datatype. The abstract key should contain lookup keywords. To provide the best possible access, index this column.

Since the abstract key is searched in keyword scans, the *text* field will not be accessed for filtering. This cost saving could be enormous, for in the current and System 10.x releases, *text* pages flow through the data cache. As these pages populate the data cache, they cause other, potentially frequently-accessed pages to exit the cache. This can dramatically alter the data cache effectiveness in on-line transaction processing (OLTP) environments.

# Epilogue

*The following list summarizes the tasks performed as you added derived columns to tables, based on the values of, or existence of values in, other columns in other tables.*

❶ Identified critical database transactions that rely on recurring calculations for which the underlying data does not change often.

❷ Added derived columns to suitable tables.

❸ Considered adding columns for use as indexes for text data.

## *Some things to remember:*

▶ Derived data which is updated often and read infrequently may be better maintained through a view access which incorporates the derivation algorithm in the results.

▶ Adding a derived column will increase the table's size, allowing fewer rows per data page. Recalculate your table size accordingly.

▶ The derived column will require integrity maintenance such as a trigger which could cause a performance penalty, particularly when the derived column is highly volatile.

▶ Consider using a derived *varchar* column to support indexing on a *text* column. Using the *varchar* will save your data cache from text page wash.

# Chapter 6
## Collapsing Tables

## Prologue

*In this chapter, you will combine two or more tables into one table.*

### Must you do this activity? Why or when?

Yes, when the application must frequently access data in multiple tables in a single query.

### What do you need before you start? How or where do you get it?

- List of critical transactions you derived from Chapter 3.
- Table and column definitions.
- Naming conventions.

### What are the tasks in this activity?

① Specify transactions that often require a significant portion of the data from more than one table, especially those with one-to-one relationships.

② Collapse tables to improve the performance of those transactions.

## *Some things to keep in mind*

■ When you collapse tables in a parent-child relationship, you must repeat the columns from the parent for each child record. Keep an accounting of these changes so that you can specify the integrity of this repeated data, in Chapter 17.

■ Performance testing may require:
- further collapsing of tables or
- decomposing collapsed tables.

# Tasks_____

*Read through all the tasks in this section before you begin the first task. Perform tasks sequentially, as presented.*

## ① *Identifying Transactions*

When normalizing your *logical* database model, you broke down entities to provide minimum redundancy of data. The decomposition of parent–child relationships into two tables may not be optimal for certain query operations.

If you expect that queries which refer to the majority of columns in both the parent and child tables might not meet the required response time, then you should collapse the tables they reference.

## ② *Collapsing or Combining Tables*

You can use this technique to generate a new table that contains one record for each parent–child record combination. Performance improves the most when the parent columns are not volatile, and your application queries consistently access a large set of rows.

For example, in the pubs sample database, if a critical request joins a number of columns in both the titles table and the publishers table, and the SQL is not meeting performance requirements, then try collapsing or combining the two tables, as in the example in Figure 6.1.

The major disadvantages of table collapse are:

- The overhead of maintaining duplicate copies of parent data for each corresponding child record. You must place an *update* trigger on the new table to maintain redundant fields previously stored in the parent table. Thus, table collapse may severely impede performance of *update* transactions.

- The extra storage costs of storing redundant information.

- The performance degradation of SQL operations which do not refer to the majority of columns in the collapsed table. This is caused by the large amount of I/O involved in scanning a greater number of rows.

Figure 6.1 Collapsing tables example ------------------------------------------------------

```
┌──────────────────────────┐
│ titles                   │
│                          │
├──────────────────────────┤
│ title_id                 │
│ title                    │
│ type                     │
│ pub_id                   │
│ price                    │
│ advance                  │
│ total_sales              │
│ notes                    │
│ pubdate                  │
│ contract                 │
│ pubname                  │
│ city                     │
│ state                    │
└──────────────────────────┘
```

*Combining the publishers and titles tables will improve the performance of the critical query. However, you must maintain the duplicate publisher information.*

# Epilogue

*The following list summarizes the tasks performed as you collapsed tables.*

❶ Specified transactions that often require a significant portion of the data from more than one table, especially those with one-to-one relationships.

❷ Collapsed tables to improve the performance of those transactions.

## Some things to remember:

▶ You must place an *update* trigger on the new or modified table to maintain redundant columns previously stored in the parent table.

▶ Other operations which did not use the parent data may suffer due to the increased number of I/O's necessary to obtain these larger rows from the Server.

# Chapter 7
## *Splitting Tables*

## Prologue

*In this chapter, you will partition a table into two or more disjoint tables. Partitioning may be horizontal (row-wise), vertical (column-wise), or mixed.*

**Must you do this activity? Why or when?**

Yes, when it is more advantageous to access a subset of data, and no important transactions rely on a consolidated view of the data.

**What do you need before you start? How or where do you get it?**

- List of critical transactions you derived from Chapter 3.
- Table and column definitions.
- Primary-key definitions.
- Naming conventions.

**What are the tasks in this activity?**

① Identify candidate tables based on critical database transactions.

② Split the table based on usage into horizontal table splits or vertical table splits.

③ Consider mixed fragmentation.

### *Some things to keep in mind*

■ You must inform application developers of the new table names and the new relationships of the data.

■ When you split tables vertically, keep an accounting of the changes so that you can address maintenance of the keys, in Chapter 17.

■ Performance testing may require:
- further splitting of tables or
- collapsing of the split tables.

# Tasks

*Read through all the tasks in this section before you begin the first task.*
*Perform tasks sequentially, as presented.*

## ① *Identifying Candidate Tables Based on Critical Database Transactions*

In physical database design, you may decide to split a logical entity into two or more tables to improve performance and availability. This technique has various names: Table Splitting, Table Partitioning, Data Fragmentation, Segmenting Tables, Over-normalization.

To find likely candidates for this activity, consider any table used by a critical transaction that very frequently or very infrequently accesses a subset of the table's columns. Similarly, consider any table used by a critical transaction that very frequently or very infrequently accesses a subset of the table's rows.

## ② *Splitting the Table According to Usage*

You fragment a table by partitioning it into a minimal number of disjoint sub-tables (fragments). These fragments contain enough information to reconstruct the original table. The two different schemes for fragmenting a table are: horizontal and vertical.

### Horizontal table splits

Horizontal fragmentation partitions the rows of a table into disjoint subsets. The result is a set of tables with the same columns but with a different set of rows in each table. The global table is reconstructed by the union of all the horizontal fragments.

**WARNING!**
Horizontal fragments must not overlap. Overlapping horizontal fragments are too difficult to analyze and maintain.

## Figure 7.1 Supplier table example ---------------------------------------------------

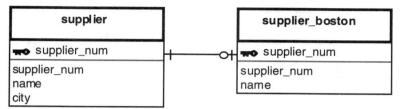

You can form horizontal fragments of the table in Figure 7.1 based on values of the city column.

For instance, fragment supplier_boston is formed by:

```
select * from supplier
where city = "Boston"
```

In some cases, you cannot base horizontal fragmentation of a table on a property of its own attributes, but must derive it from horizontal fragmentation of another table. Consider the tables shown in Figure 7.2.

You can partition the table in Figure 7.2 so that a fragment contains rows for suppliers in a given city. The fragment "supply_boston" is defined as:

```
select * from supply, supplier
where supply.supplier_num = supplier.supplier_num
and supplier.city = "Boston"
```

Horizontal table splitting is very useful in the following circumstances:

- A table is large and reducing its size reduces the number of index pages read in a query.
- The table split corresponds to an actual physical separation of the data rows, as in different geographical sites.
- Table splitting achieves specific distribution of data on the available physical media.

**WARNING!**
Horizontal fragmentation splits the data rows of a table. You must define logic in your application to locate a particular data row.

## Figure 7.2 Horizontal fragmentation example -------------------------------------------

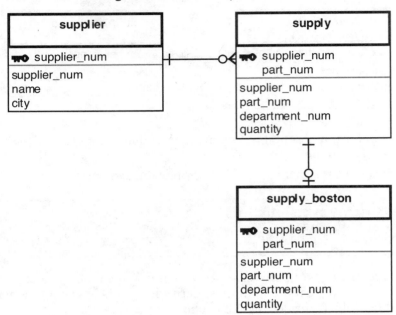

## Vertical table splits

Vertical fragmentation partitions the columns of a table. Each fragment must include the primary key of the rows of the table. The global table is reconstructed by joining the two fragments via the primary key. Vertical fragmentation frequently separates accessed data from data that is rarely accessed.

Consider the employee table in Figure 7.3.

If an application accesses salary and tax data less frequently than it accesses other biographical information, then the two vertical fragments for the employee table are as shown in Figure 7.4.

Vertical table splitting is very useful in the following circumstances:

- A subset of the columns in a table are accessed frequently.

- Two critical transactions accessing the table have widely varying range searches. This can be resolved by splitting the table vertically and having a clustered index on each new resulting table, each one specific to the needs of one of the critical transactions.

Figure 7.3 Employee table example --------------------------------------------------------

Figure 7.4 Employee table vertical split example ---------------------------------------

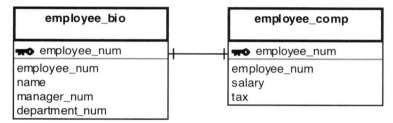

- The table has wide rows. Splitting the table causes smaller rows. This allows many more rows to be stored on each data page, therefore increasing performance efficiency for critical queries.

- The table has such wide rows that every data page contains a large amount of unusable space (since the space is large but not large enough to hold an entire row.) Splitting the rows promotes more efficient space utilization.

**WARNING!**

Vertical fragmentation splits the columns of a table. You must define logic in your application to access a particular column.

## ③ *Considering Mixed Fragmentation*

Mixed fragmentation is the result of the successive application of both fragmentation techniques: horizontal and vertical.

In the earlier vertical fragmentation example of the employee table, you can achieve mixed fragmentation by doing horizontal fragmentation of the two vertical fragments based on department_num.

# Epilogue

*The following list summarizes the tasks performed as you partitioned a table into two or more disjoint tables.*

❶ Identified candidate tables based on critical database transactions.

❷ Split the table based on usage into horizontal table splits or vertical table splits.

❸ Considered mixed fragmentation.

## *Some things to remember:*

▶ Horizontal fragments must not overlap since they are too difficult to implement and to subsequently analyze.

▶ Horizontal fragments split the data rows of a table; therefore, you must define logic either in stored procedures or in your application program which can locate a particular row in the correct table.

▶ Similarly, vertical fragments split the columns of a table and you must therefore define logic elsewhere which can locate the correct table for a particular column.

# Chapter 8
# *Handling Supertypes and Subtypes*

## Prologue_____

*In this chapter, you will decide how to implement tables involved in a supertype/subtype relationship in the logical data model.*

**Must you do this activity? Why or when?**
- Read through all the tasks in this section before you begin the first task. Perform tasks sequentially, as presented.
- Yes, if the logical data model contains supertype and subtype entities.

**What do you need before you start? How or where do you get it?**
- Table and column definitions.
- Primary-key definitions.
- Knowledge and understanding of critical database transactions and their performance requirements.
- Naming conventions.

**What are the tasks in this activity?**
① Identify tables in a supertype/subtype relationship in the data model.
② Identify and analyze the transactions accessing the supertype and sub-type tables.
③ Determine the best way to handle supertype/subtype relationships.

## *Some things to keep in mind*

■ After performance testing, you may need to reassess choices made to implement a supertype/subtype relationship.

■   Keep an accounting of your changes to tables so that you can handle the integrity among the new or modified tables in Chapter 17, "Maintaining Derived and Redundant Data."

# Tasks

*Read through all the tasks in this section before you begin the first task. Perform tasks sequentially, as presented.*

These tasks will help you to determine which of the three possible solutions to use in handling supertypes and subtypes:

- Single supertype table which contains columns in common and multiple subtype tables containing differentiating columns
- Single supertype table containing all columns
- One table for each subtype containing columns unique to the subtype and the columns in common with the other subtypes

## ①  *Identifying Supertype/Subtype Tables*

Some entities and their relationships are best modeled by a subtype/supertype relationship in the logical database design. A supertype entity contains all the columns that are common to all subtype entities. A subtype entity contains columns to support the more specific requirements of the subtype. Each subtype has a primary key that is the same as that of the supertype. However, each subtype entity usually has its own attributes and participates in relationships different from those of the supertype.

Subtypes and supertypes are not typically part of the semantics of a relational database management system. This section tells you how to develop a physical database design reflecting the concepts found in subtypes and supertypes.

The following example, Entity Relationship Diagram (ERD), in Figure 8.1 shows entities from the logical design (or an earlier stage of physical design) and is the starting point for the examples in this section.

When identifying supertype/subtype relationships which may exist in your logical design, you should determine whether:

- subtypes have a few differences and many common attributes; or
- subtypes have many differences and few common attributes.

48

Figure 8.1 Logical design starting point ----------------------------------------------

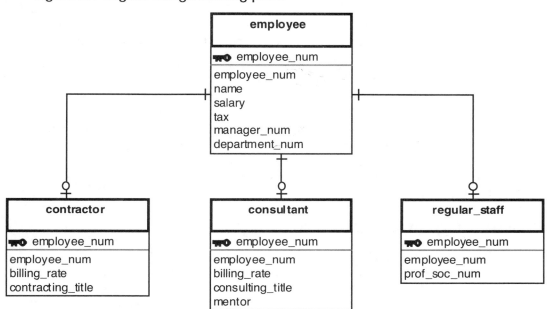

## ② *Identifying and Analyzing Transactions*

Analyze the transactions which use these supertype/subtype entities by determining whether:

- subtype data is accessed independently and other data accessed jointly.
- subtype data is accessed independently and the rows are wide.
- subtype data is accessed at the same time.

The more active and wide the data contained within the table's rows, the less likely the database design is to support the use of a supertype table. In addition, the multi-user environment directly affects supertype access. Simultaneously accessed subtype columns are best separated, if possible, into multiple subtypes.

## Advantages of supertype tables

Performance is often better with one large supertype table, because fewer joins are required to retrieve all information for a given entity. Since there are no foreign keys to maintain, referential integrity is not a performance issue. Finally, in some cases, a simple design with few tables may suffice.

## Advantages of subtype tables

Use subtype tables if performance of transactions against these tables is expected to be non-critical or sufficient, since these tables ensure no "inapplicable" nulls.

Subtype tables are smaller. They call for additional key values, but fewer null values. The tables are smaller, so performance may be better for certain queries.

Design stability is the most important advantage of separate subtype tables. Any new attribute applicable to only one subtype requires changes to only one table design. By contrast, storing all attributes in a single supertype might require additional programming to ensure that the column holds a value only for a specific subtype.

# ③ *Handling Supertypes and Subtypes*

In the physical database design, you should include tables for each logical supertype entity and each subtype entity. An additional attribute in the supertype table determines which subtype table is appropriate for a given instance. The subtype tables contain only the attributes which are appropriate for the specific subtype. This physical design has fewest null values.

There are three common physical designs based on the supertype/subtype paradigm. Which one is best for your database depends on data activity against the table(s) and the frequency or concurrency of *select*s, *update*s, and *delete*s as they occur against data.

The three common physical design scenarios for subtypes and supertypes are:

- One supertype and multiple subtypes, which become a collection of tables represented conceptually by a table containing all columns in common and one or more tables with specific columns unique to that table, all sharing the same primary key.

- One supertype and one or more subtypes, which are combined into a single table.

- Two or more subtypes and no supertype, which become multiple specific tables sharing the same primary key.

## Single supertype table and multiple subtype tables

In Figure 8.2, common attributes of employees are stored in the employee table. The employee table has an additional attribute—employee_type—which determines the appropriate subtable for the employee.

Figure 8.2 Single supertype/multiple subtype example-----------------------------

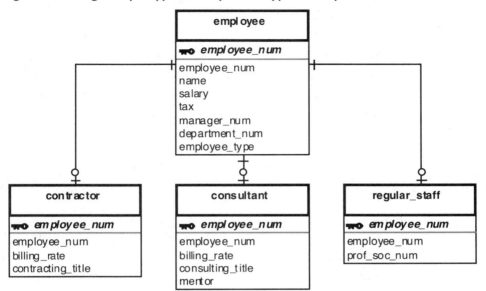

All tables have the same primary key. All attributes for a specific type of employee are retrieved by joining the supertype table and subtype tables on the primary key.

Use this technique when the subtypes have many differences and few common attributes and reports rarely require the supertype data with the subtype data. Additionally, this technique is useful when the number of subtypes is initially unknown. Adding a new subtype does not alter existing tables' definitions. Furthermore, if only new applications need knowledge of the new subtype, existing applications need not alter their access mechanisms.

## Single supertype table

An alternative physical design merges subtype tables with the supertype table. This creates a very wide table because all columns from all subtype tables are included, with many null values. This is a specific case of combining tables horizontally. Combining tables may have the advantages of better performance and simple access.

This technique is appropriate if the subtypes:

- have similar columns
- are involved in similar relationships

- are frequently referenced together
- are infrequently accessed separately

Other reasons to combine the supertype table with the subtype tables include:

- the supertype and subtypes are usually accessed together
- the supertype and subtypes are infrequently accessed separately
- the effect on performance, data availability, and storage is acceptable

Since not all attributes will pertain to all row occurrences, it is sometimes impractical to have separate subtype tables. Further, problems may arise with maintenance and integrity enforcement.

In Figure 8.3, a single supertype table is chosen for these reasons:

- one sector of the organization frequently generates personnel reports not used by any other organization
- there are seldom contractors or consultants on the payroll
- the title of "contractor" or "consultant" applies to every employee and cannot be separated out of the main record
- there are extensive nulls in the individual rows

Figure 8.3 Single supertype table example ----------------------------------------------

| employee |
| --- |
| ⏦● employee_num |
| employee_num |
| name |
| salary |
| tax |
| manager_num |
| department_num |
| consulting_title |
| contracting_title |
| billing_rate |
| mentor |
| prof_soc_num |
| employee_type |

## Subtype tables only

Choose this design scenario if a supertype entity in the logical database design existed only to clarify concepts or to add clarity to the model. Your physical database design can omit a table for the supertype if it adds no new information and is not referenced in any known data requests. If the supertype entity has no attributes other than the primary key, one of these aforementioned situations is true. All data that is part of the supertype is accessed by the union of all the subtype tables.

Specify subtype-based tables if the data has a high frequency of access, with multiple updates.

In Figure 8.4, no common attributes are stored for different types of employees. The union of all subtype tables will return data on all employees.

## Figure 8.4 Subtype tables only example ----------------------------------------------

| contractor |
| --- |
| 🔑 employee_num |
| employee_num |
| billing_rate |
| contracting_title |
| name |
| salary |
| tax |
| manager_num |
| department_num |

| consultant |
| --- |
| 🔑 employee_num |
| employee_num |
| billing_rate |
| consulting_title |
| mentor |
| name |
| salary |
| tax |
| manager_num |
| department_num |

| regular_staff |
| --- |
| 🔑 employee_num |
| employee_num |
| prof_soc_num |
| name |
| salary |
| tax |
| manager_num |
| department_num |

# Epilogue _____

*The following list summarizes the tasks performed as you decided how to implement tables involved in a supertype/subtype relationship in the logical data model.*

❶ Identified tables in a supertype/subtype relationship in the data model.

❷ Identified and analyzed the transactions accessing the supertype and subtype tables.

❸ Determined the best way to handle supertype/subtype relationships:

• Single supertype table containing columns in common andmultiple subtype tables containing differentiating columns

- Single supertype table containing all columns
- One table for each subtype containing columns unique to thesub-type and the columns in common with the other subtypes

## *Some things to remember:*

▶ Consider using one supertype table and many subtype tables when the subtypes have many differences and few common attributes and reports rarely require the supertype data with the subtype data.

▶ Consider using a single supertype table when the subtypes have few differences and many common attributes, and when you must report many of the subtypes together or must frequently report the supertype attributes and subtypes together.

▶ Consider using only subtype tables if the supertype attributes are few and are never or rarely used independently.

# Chapter 9
## *Duplicating Parts of Tables*

## Prologue

*In this chapter, you will duplicate data vertically (columns) and/or horizontally (rows) into new tables.*

**Must you do this activity? Why or when?**

Yes, when it is more advantageous to access a subset of data in some transactions and provide a consolidated view of the data for other transactions.

**What do you need before you start? How or where do you get it?**

• List of critical transactions you derived from Chapter 3.

• Table and column definitions.

• Primary-key definitions.

• Naming conventions.

**What are the tasks in this activity?**

① Identify transactions where a subset of a table is frequently accessed, and there is a concurrent requirement for a consolidated view of the data which cannot tolerate a join.

② Create new tables to hold duplicated data.

### *Some things to keep in mind*

■ Duplicating parts of a table may result in data integrity problems. To prevent these, keep an accounting of any duplications, so that you can handle mechanisms to maintain integrity in Chapter 17, "Maintaining Derived and Redundant Data."

■ Applications will need to know which table to access.

■ Performance testing may require further duplication of tables or elimination of tables created to duplicate data.

# Tasks

*Read through all the tasks in this section before you begin the first task. Perform tasks sequentially, as presented.*

## ① *Identifying Transaction Domains*

Duplicated tables are useful when data is oriented more toward decision-support-oriented than OLTP; that is, the OLTP application can benefit from having its data independently accessible from the decision-support data .

This technique is useful for a transaction that routinely accesses parts of a table for some processing and routinely accesses the entire table for other processing.

Consider the case of a catalog house order-processing system. The catalog house has observed that 90% of their orders come from customers who have ordered merchandise within the past year. The catalog house maintains customer information for a period of five years and routinely sends marketing promotion literature to their entire customer base. Duplicating part of the customer table will facilitate order entry.

## ② *Creating Tables for Duplicated Data*

You must first define the vertical and/or horizontal cuts on the primary data copies. Then you create a new table to contain the required data.

Duplicate tables are smaller than the primary tables. The smaller duplicate table:

- Shrinks the size of indexes, for horizontally duplicated data. The smaller index structure reduces the number of logical I/Os required to traverse the B-Tree.

- Reduces the number of logical I/Os required to process vertically duplicated data. This reduction occurs because eliminating columns increases the number of rows per data page, and more rows can be retrieved in one logical I/O operation.

# Epilogue

*The following list summarizes the tasks performed as you duplicated data vertically (columns) and/or horizontally (rows) into new tables.*

❶ Identified transactions where a subset of a table is frequently accessed, and there is a concurrent requirement for a consolidated view of the data which cannot tolerate a join.

❷ Created new tables to hold duplicated data.

## *Some things to remember:*

▶ Because a duplicate table is smaller than the primary table, horizontally duplicated data will lead to smaller indexes, reducing the number of logical I/Os necessary to traverse the B-Tree for an entry.

▶ For vertically duplicated data, the number of logical I/Os for the data pages is reduced since more rows can now fit on a single data page.

# Chapter 10
## *Adding Tables for Derived Data*

## Prologue_____

*In this chapter, you will create new tables, which hold data derived from columns in other tables.*

**Must you do this activity? Why or when?**

Yes, when the structure of the database does not support commonly accessed information, and the derived data does not naturally fit in an existing table.

**What do you need before you start? How or where do you get it?**

- List of critical transactions you derived from Chapter 3.
- Table and column definitions.
- Naming conventions.

**What are the tasks in this activity?**

① Identify transactions that require a new structure for derived data.

② Create new table(s) to hold derived data and to hold other columns that may be needed for reporting purposes.

### *Some things to keep in mind*

■ You must maintain derived data any time the underlying data is changed. Keep an accounting of any new tables so that you can handle maintenance of the derived data, in Chapter 17, "Maintaining Derived and Redundant Data."

■ Performance testing may require:
- creating other new tables
- redesigning the tables you created
- eliminating the tables you created

# Tasks

*Read through all the tasks in this section before you begin the first task. Perform tasks sequentially, as presented.*

## ① *Identifying Transactions*

Most applications or reports call for data summaries, often at more than one level of grouping for the same source data.

Generating summaries, particularly with large tables, may become a performance bottleneck, due to the sheer volume of records being processed. It also requires many I/O operations and CPU resources.

Generating a summary table can help you remove the bottleneck and obtain summaries within the required time.

When you consider using summary tables, remember:

- The summary tables will consume disk resources for indexes and table pages.
- The summary tables need to be maintained. If any changes are made to the underlying data representing the group criteria or summarized columns, then the summary row will need to be rebuilt. This operation can be quite costly if the referenced fields are volatile.

A summary table can also be useful when you need explosion tables for data analysis. Explosion tables hold detailed information derived from data in other tables.

## ② *Creating Tables for Derived Data*

When you create tables to hold derived data, consider using either an explosion table or a summary table as explained next.

### Explosion tables

An explosion table is comprised of data derived from existing data which has been altered by a particular business algorithm. It maintains the data in an exploded or altered form from the standard storage representation.

Consider a financial analysis database containing annualized data on market trends. Even though the data is available only on an annualized basis, the application needs to report on seasonal patterns. You can use an algorithm to explode the table containing annualized data, store the derived data in a new table, and perform seasonal-pattern reporting from the new table.

## Summary tables

A summary table contains the columns that represent the group condition, as well as the columns that represent aggregate or summary data. It provides better performance than if SQL generates the summary data.

For example, if critical SQL queries on the titles table produce a report on the year-to-date sales of books by book type, and performance is not going to be met, consider storing this pre-computed information in a summary table, like the one shown in Figure 10.1.

**Figure 10.1 Summary table example**----------------------------------------------------

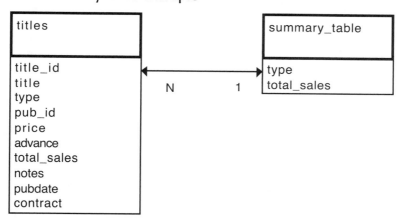

The titles summary_table contains one column named type for the book type grouping condition, and one column total_sales to hold the total sales for the given book type. You must add or modify triggers to update the summary_table upon changes to the titles table, or plan to perform updates through time-based processing.

# Epilogue _____

*The following list summarizes the tasks performed as you created new tables, which hold data derived from columns in other tables.*

❶ Identified transactions that require a new structure for derived data.

❷ Created new table(s) to hold derived data and to hold other columns that may be needed for reporting purposes.

# Chapter 11
## *Handling Vector Data*

## Prologue

*In this chapter, you will decide how to implement tables that contain plural attributes (vector data). Plural attributes may be implemented in a row-wise or column-wise fashion.*

**Must you do this activity? Why or when?**

Yes, if your data model contains tables with plural attributes.

**What do you need before you start? How or where do you get it?**

- List of critical transactions you derived from Chapter 3.

- Table and column definitions.

- Naming conventions.

**What are the tasks in this activity?**

① Identify tables containing plural attributes.

② Determine whether any critical transactions access tables with plural attributes.

③ Determine the best way to handle plural attributes.

## Tasks

*Read through all the tasks in this section before you begin the first task. Perform tasks sequentially, as presented.*

## ① *Identifying Tables with Plural Attributes*

A vector is a plural attribute, where the number of values is always the same.

For example, an American university may track enrollment at the freshman, sophomore, junior, and senior levels. Since each year has exactly five enrollment figures—one to label the year and one for each of the four levels—enrollment is a vector.

Another example is the data for a custom tailoring shop. The tailor shop needs to keep track of customer measurements such as sleeve length, shoulder breadth, waist, and inseam. Since the number of measurements for each customer is always the same, measurement is a plural attribute.

## ② *Identifying Transactions*

You can store vector data in a row-wise or column-wise fashion, as explained in the next section. How you should store the data depends on how the data needs to be accessed and reported. If the application routinely needs to report the data in a tabular format, then a row-wise design is probably more appropriate. Otherwise, consider a column-wise design.

## ③ *Handling Plural Attributes*

Vectors can be implemented either row-wise or column-wise. In the row-wise example shown in Figure 11.1, each year occupies a row and each of the five levels occupies a separate column. In the column-wise example, all enrollment figures go in a single column.

### Figure 11.1 Row-wise vector data example -------------------------------------------

| year | freshman | sophomore | junior | senior |
|------|----------|-----------|--------|--------|
| 1990 | 200 | 125 | 122 | 100 |
| 1991 | 207 | 198 | 175 | 175 |
| 1992 | 172 | 168 | 166 | 160 |

## Row-wise design implementation

A row-wise table implementation has some advantages. First, it is usually more compact. In the column-wise table, each enrollment figure requires an additional class name, year, and internal row header. This could multiply your need for physical storage. Physical overhead is much lower in the row-wise table, probably only a few bytes per enrollment figure. However, if data is missing or unknown, the row-wise design fills with some nulls and is relatively less efficient.

Another advantage of row-wise design is that you need fewer tables. Usually an entity has singular attributes in addition to the plural attributes. For example, your model may also include tuition for each year. This singular attribute fits well in the row-wise table as another column. In a column-wise design, tuition causes redundancy, so you must specify an additional table, leading to additional joins and additional foreign keys.

### WARNING!

A row-wise design can be unworkable when there is no reasonable limit on the number of values since this can lead to either extremely large or widely varying sizes.

A row-wise design may yield another advantage: user comprehensibility. The row-wise table looks familiar (like a spreadsheet) and may be easier for ad hoc query users to work with than a column-wise table, which requires the user to write the N-way self-join.

## Column-wise design implementation

A column-wise implementation is the natural relational design and is really required for plural attributes that are not vectors. If you cannot determine whether a plural attribute is a vector, use a column-wise design; see the example in Figure 11.2.

What if the vector changes in size? In the university example, if a user decides to track master's and doctoral enrollment, a row-wise design requires you to add new columns and, probably, to change the application software. A column-wise design allows for the values to change without a schema modification. Also, any application software changes which might be necessary are typically less complex. Unless you are facing a very expensive difference in storage requirements, the benefits of a stable design can be significant.

Another big advantage of a column-wise design is its compatibility with Transact-SQL functions. Average enrollment is easy to compute with an *avg()* function against a column-wise design, but the Transact-SQL is not straightforward for a row-wise table. This difference is especially important when you consider changing vector size. The column-wise average is still accurate, but you must rewrite a row-wise query.

Figure 11.2 Column-wise vector data example -----------------------------------------

| year | class | enrollment |
|------|-------|------------|
| 1990 | freshman | 200 |
| 1990 | sophomore | 125 |
| 1990 | junior | 122 |
| 1990 | senior | 100 |
| 1991 | freshman | 207 |
| 1991 | sophomore | 198 |
| 1991 | junior | 175 |
| 1991 | senior | 175 |
| 1992 | freshman | 172 |
| 1992 | sophomore | 168 |
| 1992 | junior | 166 |
| 1992 | senior | 160 |

# Epilogue

*The following list summarizes the tasks performed as you decided how to implement tables that contained plural attributes (vector data).*

❶ Identified tables containing plural attributes.

❷ Determined whether any critical transactions access tables with plural attributes.

❸ Determined the best way to handle plural attributes, either a row-wise design or a column-wise design.

## Some things to remember:

▶ A row-wise design is unworkable when there is no reasonable limit on the number of values.

▶ A row-wise design looks familiar and may be easier to use for ad hoc queries.

▶ Column-wise is the natural relational design and is really required for plural attributes that are not vectors.

# Chapter 12
## *Generating Sequence Numbers*

## Prologue

*In this chapter, you will choose a strategy to generate sequence numbers; then create the appropriate tables and columns to support the strategy.*

**Must you do this activity? Why or when?**

Yes, if your database uses sequence numbers.

**What do you need before you start? How or where do you get it?**

- List of critical transactions you derived from Chapter 3.
- Complete table and column definitions.
- Primary-key definitions.
- Naming conventions.

**What are the tasks in this activity?**

① Identify tables that contain sequence numbers.

② Identify and analyze transactions that add to or modify the sequence numbers in these tables.

③ Choose from among five strategies for generating and storing sequence numbers.

### *Some things to keep in mind*

■ Performance testing may suggest other strategy choices.

## Tasks

*Read through all the tasks in this section before you begin the first task. Perform tasks sequentially, as presented.*

# ① *Identifying Tables that Contain Sequence Numbers*

You can use sequence numbers to uniquely identify tables, rows, or columns in a database. Most often, they are used as unique identifiers for row data. For example, sequence numbers can serve as invoice numbers, employee numbers, record numbers, etc.

Sequence numbers are beneficial in several different situations. They are mostly used to identify surrogate keys.

# ② *Identifying Transactions that Affect Sequence Numbers*

It is important to know how frequently new sequence numbers are being inserted into the tables. This knowledge comes from analyzing the transactions which insert new sequence numbers in these tables. The strategy chosen depends on the rate and frequency of inserts.

# ③ *Choosing the Best Sequence-Number Strategy*

You will be choosing from five strategies for generating and storing sequence numbers:

- Dynamic generation
- One column per sequence number
- One table per sequence number
- One row per sequence number
- SQL Server 10.x *identity* feature

## Dynamic generation using current maximum

The most common method for generating sequence numbers is to create a transaction that increments by one the current maximum value of a particular column, then selects the number that has been generated, using the number as the identifier for the row to be inserted. The method described next forces the transaction to acquire what is referred to as an exclusive lock on the table immediately by placing a generic *update* statement at the beginning of the transaction.

**Note**
This strategy is appropriate for low-volume insert activity only.

For example, suppose you are maintaining an employee identification field (emp_id) as a unique identifier and index for an employee table. Each time a new employee needs to be inserted into a table, a new sequence number is generated as follows:

```
declare @maxid int
begin transaction
    update employee set emp_id = 1where 1=2
    select @maxid = 1 + max(emp_id)
        from employee
    insert into employee values(@maxid,...)
commit transaction
```

If User A begins the transaction, User B is not allowed access to the table until User A's transaction is complete. No deadlock can occur, and the sequence value is properly inserted.

Some things to consider:

- You should put this transaction in a stored procedure, so that any application that inserts records into the employee table updates the sequence number (emp_id) accordingly.

- To maintain this field during deletions and updates—particularly if the field is used as a foreign key in another table—you must specify triggers. (Note: this may cause a performance penalty. If you *insert* a row in the foreign key table, leaving the id field null, the transaction will, in the end, have to actually perform 2 *inserts* and a *delete*, once it has performed the *update* of the id field. However, other alternatives may be more costly.)

- There may be some performance degradation with this method since it places an exclusive lock on the entire table. Use this technique only when you expect insert activity to be infrequent.

- If you think that the sequence number value may exceed the maximum possible positive integer value for an *int* datatype (2,147,483,647), consider alternatives such as using a SQL Server 10.x *numeric* with 0 scale, a *float*, or a *double precision* datatype. However, recall that these numbers are approximate datatypes. The actual rounded value stored by SQL Server will depend on the specific machine-dependent rounding algorithm of the Server's platform.

- You may also use a modulo arithmetic operator (%) between the incremented sequence value and the maximum integer value. Such a technique causes the sequence to automatically recycle to zero once the maximum value has been reached. To avoid a sequence number of zero, always add 1 to the result of the modulo function:

```
update employee
    set emp_id = (emp_id % 2,147,483,647) + 1
```

Be sure that the initial setting of emp_id is 1 or greater. A zero value would cause the integer overflow you are trying to avoid!

- Create a clustered index on the id column so that you can obtain the *max* value quickly, though this index may cause some contention on the first and last data page if your insert rate is high.

- Create a nonclustered index on the id column so that you can take advantage of index covering. Such an index is not an obvious gain since you have transferred page contention from the data page to the index page. Furthermore, any other extenuating factors such as triggers, etc. may prevent the update-in-place to occur.

- Use a *fillfactor* value when creating indexes so that data and index pages have sufficient spare real estate to ensure that the insertion of a new row will not require allocation of a new page.

- Put this transaction into a trigger that updates the emp_id each time a new record is inserted.

## One column per sequence number

Design a table in which one row contains next-available sequence numbers that correspond to all the tables. For an example, see Figure 12.1.

Use this technique when the overhead associated with one table per sequence number (16 KBytes) threatens your space management; for example, if you have 100 sequence numbers to track, but have a low insert rate, you may not want to give up 100 * 16 KBytes of space to track them.

Figure 12.1 One column per sequence number example ---------------------------

| titles | authors | publishers |
|--------|---------|------------|
| 3569   | 2234    | 3246       |

This design facilitates systems where many tables receive new rows because data comes in from an outside process. This design lets you get all the needed sequence numbers from only one row.

The problem with this type of design is that if your database changes—if for example, you add another table—you must add another column to this table, which would be much more tedious than adding another row. This method can also cause needless contention, as transactions needing sequence numbers for different tables compete for the same data page. Consider a scenario where transaction A ends up locking out transaction B, even though A wanted the sequence number for the employee table, and B wanted the sequence number for the order table.

## One table per sequence number

A method that avoids the contention problem is to have separate tables, each containing the sequence number for a particular table. See Figure 12.2 for an example. This prevents problems with access but can be difficult to maintain. This strategy is appropriate for high-volume insertion activity.

Figure 12.2 One table per sequence number example ----------------------------

titles table:

| sequence_number |
|-----------------|
| 3569            |

authors table:

| sequence_number |
|-----------------|
| 2234            |

publishers table:

| sequence_number |
|-----------------|
| 3246            |

**WARNING!**
Since each table in a database reserves 8 pages of memory upon creation, this option uses the most space overhead, requiring 16 KBytes of memory to be reserved for each sequence number, as well as the pages for the clustered index, if you are trying to guarantee update-in-place.

## One row per sequence number

Another method for generating sequence numbers is to create a table containing one row for each table in the database. Each row contains the table name and the sequence number used for inserting the next row. For an example of this, see Figure 12.3.

Figure 12.3 One row per sequence number example---------------------------------

| table_name | sequence_number |
|------------|-----------------|
| titles     | 3569            |
| authors    | 2234            |
| publishers | 3246            |

A given application, upon preparing to insert a row in a sequential table, queries the table_name table in Figure 12.3 and gets the next available sequence number, increments it, and inserts a new sequence number into the table. This approach skips the step, used in the nested-transaction strategy, of searching the sequential table for a maximum value. However, you must provide triggers or stored procedures to keep the separate table_name table updated.

The disadvantage is that you must look for this value in another table and this value must be maintained through the use of triggers and stored procedures.

If the insertion activity is high, the table holding the next available sequence numbers can become a bottleneck. Concurrency is likely to be poor because the rows of the table are short, and so locking a page locks many rows, probably all of them. To avoid this, you can pad the rows with dummy columns, using *char(255)* columns as necessary to make the row greater than 1012 bytes. Finally, you can use an index *fillfactor* to disperse the rows.

## Locking issues with application-generated sequence numbers

With any of the four options above, it is possible that while a sequence number is being updated and a new record inserted, another application may access the same available sequence number and try to insert a different record with an identical key.

The following example brings together locking concerns and setup for a table with one row per sequence number. It first creates the table which will hold all sequence counters and creates a unique clustered index on the column that identifies the row. (You may choose to use a column, key_name *char(x)*, in place of counter_id, which would hold the application name instead of a number to identify the row.) The SQL next determines what the current maximum value is in the existing data of the associated user table. Finally, it obtains a new sequence number to be used for the next *insert* operation into the table.

```
create table counter (
    counter_id tinyint,
    next_count int
)
go


create unique clustered index i1 on counter
    (counter_id)
go


insert into counter
    select 1, max(col_id)
    from sample_table
go


declare @new_idint
begin transaction
    update counter
        set next_count = next_count +1
        where counter_id = 1
    select @new_id = next_count
        from counter where counter_id = 1
```

(continued)

73

```
commit transaction
select @new_id
go
```

To use this SQL for a new table, change the *insert* syntax to:

```
insert into counter
    values (1,0)
go
```

## Server-generated sequence numbers

SQL Server 10.x provides an *identity* keyword, which you can use to describe a numeric column in a table. SQL Server then maintains a sequence number for this column without any coding or intervention from you or the user. See Figure 12.4 for an example.

**Figure 12.4 Server-generated sequence numbers example**------------------------

| emp_id | emp_name | emp_addr |
|--------|----------|----------------|
| 1 | KAY | SYBASE-DENVER |
| 2 | DAVE | SYBASE-DENVER |

When creating a table, you can specify the *identity* column as follows:

```
create table employee
(emp_id numeric (4,0) identity,
emp_name char(25) not null,
emp_addr char(50) not null)
```

Notice that the identity column must be of datatype *numeric*. The identity column allows SQL Server to generate a unique identifier for the emp_id column, with a sequence number starting with 1. There is no change to the *insert* syntax. You need not specify the identity column name/value when inserting a row.

For example:

```
insert into employee values
    ("KAY", "SYBASE-DENVER")
insert into employee values
    ("DAVE", "SYBASE-DENVER")
select * from employee
```

SQL Server 10.x also maintains a global variable, @@*identity*, which may be accessed immediately after an *insert*. It contains the most recently inserted value for that field and may be accessed from any trigger or stored procedure. In the case of a stored procedure, this value is restored when the control returns to the caller. This is useful in the case of an *insert* trigger which may need to access the value of *identity* in the row just inserted.

When developing a physical design, you must determine which fields will have the *identity* property but you need not provide methods for generating these numbers. These fields may be particularly useful when defining primary and foreign keys. Remember that each table can have only one *identity* column.

**WARNING!**
When using the **bcp** utility to copy data out of a database and/or to copy data back into a database, you must be careful to specify your preference in handling the *identity* value in each row. **bcp** will either maintain the value or reset the value depending upon the options you choose.

# Epilogue

*The following list summarizes the tasks performed as you determined how to generate and store sequence numbers.*

❶ Identified tables that contain sequence numbers.

❷ Identified and analyzed transactions that add to or modify the sequence numbers in these tables.

❸ Chose from among five strategies for generating and storing sequence numbers. Which strategy is best for you would depend on what your affected critical transactions are.

- Generate sequence numbers in a nested transaction.
- Create a table holding one column for each database table, and its next available sequence number.
- Create a separate sequence-number table for each table in the database.
- Create a table holding one row for each database table, and its next available sequence number.
- Use the SQL Server 10.x *identity* feature.

## *Some things to remember:*

▶ If you choose to create a nested transaction based on the current maximum value in order to generate the next sequence number, be aware that this may cause performance degradations. This technique places an exclusive lock on the entire table in order to discover the maximum value. Use this technique only when you expect *insert* activity to be infrequent.

▶ Consider the use of a modulo on the sequence number value in order to recycle to one without overflowing the maximum value for the datatype.

▶ If you maintain all current maximums for sequence numbers in one table (either by row or by column), this maintenance table may be a bottleneck if many different processes have *insert* responsibilities.

▶ If you choose to have one maintenance table per sequence number, be forewarned that each table in a database reserves 8 data pages upon creation. Therefore, each of these tables will use up 16 KBytes just to hold one number. You may not want to choose this option if space is an issue.

▶ The SQL Server 10.x *identity* feature must be used with some caution. When using the **bcp** utility to copy data out of a database and/or to copy data back into a database, you must be careful to specify your preference in handling the *identity* value in each column. **bcp** will either maintain the value or reset it, depending on the options you indicate.

# Chapter 13
## *Specifying Indexes*

## Prologue

*In this chapter, you will specify indexes to improve data access perfor-mance, to enforce uniqueness, or to control data distribution. Indexes are placed on one or more columns of a table and may be clustered or nonclus-tered, unique or nonunique, or concatenated.*

**Must you do this activity? Why or when?**

Yes, for performance considerations or for uniqueness.

**What do you need before you start? How or where do you get it?**

- Complete table and column definitions.
- List of critical transactions you derived from Chapter 3.
- Naming conventions.

**What are the tasks in this activity?**

① Review major indexing issues.
② From the list of critical transactions, identify the individual tables and columns affected or used by the transactions.
③ Select columns that are candidates for indexes.
④ Assess the *update* patterns against the tables.
⑤ Specify a column (or columns) for the clustered index.
⑥ Specify a column (or columns) for the nonclustered indexes.

## *Some things to keep in mind*

■ Testing and trial-and-error during production may indicate other index choices.

■ Be careful not to needlessly overindex.

# Tasks

*Read through all the tasks in this section before you begin the first task. Perform tasks sequentially, as presented.*

## ① *Reviewing Indexing Issues*

Index selection is an extremely fragile exercise that depends largely on the actual access patterns exhibited by the actual processes running. You should only select indexes after you have completed transaction analysis and once you have estimated access patterns. This is vitally true since incorrect index selection can adversely affect your system's performance. Having made your selections, you can only be assured of their success, or failure, through usage and monitoring.

Your three decisions in indexing will be:

1. Do I need any indexing on this table? (Task 1)

2. If so, choose the clustered index column(s) by ranking the priority of accesses against the table. (Tasks 2, 3, and 4)

3. Now evaluate all other queries against the columns in order to choose the best nonclustered index choices. You may want to combine some columns into one nonclustered index to save space and promote index covering. (Task 5)

### Index fitness

In this process of assigning indexes and examining their usefulness, you should discover that index fitness is based more on your application query patterns than on your table definitions; the table definitions merely provide you with some hints about expected queries. Therefore, your greatest problem will be deriving the best set of indexes for your database when conflicting applications exist (i.e., applications whose access needs and priorities are in conflict). Here, you must prioritize transactions across applications to determine the best index fit. You may even discover a need to split up or duplicate a database into another database in order to support equally critical but opposing indexing strategies, particularly with respect to the clustered index, where only one is allowed per table.

## Index density and selectivity

The index density for a particular index is determined by dividing one by the number of unique values for the column or columns in the table which make up the index.

1 / Total number of unique values = Index density

For example, the index density for the unique primary key on a 5000 row table would be 1/5000 or .0002. The lower this density number is, the more selective the index is; the higher the density value, the more duplicate values exist for that index within the table. Therefore, a density value of 1.0 indicates a completely non-selective index, where all values for the index columns are identical.

The SQL Server optimizer multiplies this density number by the number of rows in the table to determine the index's selectivity, the number of rows that are expected to be accessed for a particular index value.

Index density * Total number of rows = Selectivity

The more selective (lower) this number is, the more likely the optimizer will choose to use the index since it can assume fewer iterations will be required to resolve the query. For example, .0002 * 5000 = 1, indicating that only one row should be returned for each index value.

With a composite index, the density should get lower for each additional column specified in the index, thus making the index more selective. For example, in the pubs database's authors table, an index comprised of au_lname and au_fname will have a lower density value than just au_lname because it is more selective.

Use these density and selectivity calculations to help you in determining the usefulness of a particular column or columns as an index.

## Data-value uniqueness

Indexes provide benefits above and beyond the role they play with the optimization of query plans. Indexes can enforce uniqueness of data values in the columns on which they are placed. Therefore, they are helpful integrity mechanisms, when applied to primary-key columns. With SQL Server 10.x, you can use the *primary key or unique* constraints to enforce uniqueness. Both of these constraints will cause an index to be formed for the named columns.

Consult the SYBASE SQL Server Reference Manual for further details about the constructs.

## Data distribution and contention

An index can also be used to control distribution of data across data pages. If a table has no clustered index, it is considered a heap: all inserts go to the last page of the table whether the data is ordered or not. Multiple insert processes will block one another as they await an exclusive lock on the last page. Any update of a row will move it to the end of the last page.

Similarly, sequential inserts on a table with a clustered index affect the same page. Intermediate sequential inserts (inserts on a page between the current first and last page allocated), affect the same leaf page; a page split is needed when a page becomes full. Next-highest sequential inserts (inserts on and beyond the current last page allocated), affect the last page and a new empty page to be allocated when the page is full.

Multiple processes doing the same thing in the same area may be a problem. However, keep in mind that:

1. Almost all accesses will be satisfied by the cache, and this is, in fact, a gain.

2. The lock manager must keep up with the access activity.

3. Most well-designed systems that rely on a large number of sequential inserts have relatively simple inserts; locks are therefore not held very long.

To avoid the last-page contention issue for inserting large amounts of sequential data, you can use pseudo-random keys instead of sequential keys for the indexing values. This will distribute the rows throughout the table. But then the data no longer resides in sequential order and so the time saved during insertion may be lost later in sort time if sequential-order selecting is significant.

Similarly, you may choose to have one application process perform all insert activity so that contention is no longer an issue.

**Note**

Remember that transaction analysis should indicate the priority of speedy sequential inserts versus speedy retrieval. Typically, you'll discover that this page contention issue is trivial in comparison to the gains you receive in ordering your data and in effective use of page caching.

## Index hazards

As mentioned earlier, some columns and tables may seem to meet most of the criteria for applying an index and yet it may not be suitable if the index has low selectivity. The optimizer will never choose to use the index in such a case.

When a *where* clause contains a restriction on the first column of an index, it is considered indexable; that is, the index may be used to limit the number of pages scanned to resolve the query. In such a situation, the optimizer is guaranteed to use the index. Consider the index:

```
create index idx on t (c1, c2, c3, c4, c5)
```

The *where* clause:

```
where c2 = 2 and c1 = 1
```

is considered indexable, while the *where* clause:

```
where c2 = 2 and c3 = 3
```

is not considered indexable.

In some circumstances, as in the above *where* clause, where the first column is not indicated, the optimizer may still choose to use the index; that is, while the clause is not considered indexable, the optimizer chooses to scan all the index pages versus having to scan all the data pages.

Finally, in circumstances in which the *where* clause contains the first column of the index and then a disjoint subset of the remaining columns, only the "prefix" columns are indexable. Consider the next *where* clause with respect to the previous *create index* example:

```
where c1 =1 and c3 = 3 and c4 = 4
```

Here, only the c1 restriction is considered indexable since, without a reference to column c2, the other two columns are disjoint.

To ensure that such indexes will often be beneficial to the optimizer's query plan, place the most-selected column first in the order of columns comprising an index; if there is a tie, choose the column with the most unique values. Rank any other columns you used in the index creation according to their usefulness and then place them left to right after this column within the *create index* statement.

These concatenated or composite indexes comprised of multiple columns' values may cause another indexing hazard: a very large indexing value. As key values grow in size, the number of pages required to maintain the index's B-Tree grows dramatically, especially in the case of nonclustered indexes where key values appear throughout the tree. You can handle such composite indexes more efficiently with a surrogate key. The surrogate key is typically a one-up number assigned to a row, to represent the unique value formed by its composite index. You can use this number as a foreign-key reference and the B-Tree for indexing purposes. Consider forming a surrogate key if your composite index starts to exceed 20 bytes.

When the optimizer evaluates all available indexes for a particular query, it chooses *one* index for the query plan. Therefore, don't overindex the tables of your database. Choose indexes wisely and strictly, based on the critical transactions you select in Task 2 of this activity.

Besides creating and maintaining indexes which may never be used by the optimizer, overindexing causes another, far more serious hazard. Indexes take up space, which might otherwise be used for holding data rows. Nonclustered indexes in particular require considerable space, since the B-Tree must maintain all key values within the index pages.

The final hazard to consider is the density of the index pages and data pages. If these pages are densely packed during initial creation and load of a table with a clustered index, then later inserts may frequently require SQL Server to allocate new pages and split old ones. To avoid this costly hazard during insert time, use the *fillfactor* configuration value to set a limit on how densely data pages and index pages can be packed while the index is being built. (Remember, once the index is built, this value does not affect data placement.) Such an approach can provide the best data distribution according to your system's particular needs.

## ② *Identifying Tables in Critical Transactions*

To help you determine which tables and which columns within those tables should have indexes, first consider the intent of the indexing mechanism as used by SQL Server. Essentially, the optimizer is a set of algorithms called upon to make cost-based decisions about how best to access the data required to satisfy a query; that is, it tries to minimize the cost of processing each query. Its decisions are based on several criteria, including:

- Does an index exist on this table?
- How many rows are in the table?
- How many rows qualify from the table to satisfy the query?
- If more than one table is needed to resolve the query, in what order should they be accessed?
- What is the distribution of the data values within the table?

Since indexes play such an important role in optimization, the physical database design needs to reflect a well-placed, efficient indexing scheme. Make an initial, best-guess attempt to place your indexes and then monitor your choices to ensure that they provide the benefit you had expected in optimization of queries. Very often, you'll discover a need to revisit the critical transaction issues and rebuild your indexes in slightly different, more useful ways.

Typically, the tables that you should consider as candidates for indexes are:

- tables that are used in critical transactions and that have a set of search criteria (or limited ranges) associated with them in the transaction
- tables involved in multi-table joins
- tables with a large number of rows
- tables that require enforcement of uniqueness

# ③ *Identifying Columns for Indexes*

Once you have identified the tables in critical transactions, find the columns for which indexing will provide the greatest benefit. These are:

- columns used to specify range in the *where* clause
- columns used to join one or more tables, often primary and foreign keys
- columns likely to be used as search arguments (SARGs)
- columns used to match an equijoin query
- columns used in aggregate functions
- columns used in a *group by* clause
- columns used in an *order by* clause

These tables and columns become prime candidates for indexing because of the algorithms the optimizer uses before finalizing the query plan. As stated earlier, you will only be assured of a judicious indexing decision through trial and error. Don't be afraid to try a particular index, testing its benefit against the expected access patterns.

## ④ *Assessing Update Patterns Against the Tables*

A table's indexes must be maintained with every *insert*, *update*, and *delete* operation performed on the table. Therefore, index tables with highly dynamic data only as absolutely necessary. Consider the benefits of optimization of selections versus the degradation of these three maintenance functions.

Assessing exactly what functions are performed against a table will also help you to clarify which columns should receive the clustered index and which columns, if any, should receive a nonclustered index. Additionally, it will help you resolve how to best build the nonclustered indexes.

## ⑤ *Selecting a Column (or Columns) for the Clustered Index*

The SQL Server clustered index enforces a physical ordering of the table's data within the data pages. Therefore, you apply only one, and you must apply it judiciously. This sorted order of the data is in turn accompanied by a B-Tree component that maintains a set of pointers to all the data pages used in the table.

An obvious choice for the one clustered index on a table is the table's primary key, since it will at the very least provide for uniqueness of the primary-key value. However, the primary key is not always the best choice for the clustered index. Instead, you may need to evaluate the critical transactions that might benefit from the ordering of the data based on values other than the primary key. One example is a column used to specify a range in a *where* clause.

Each time a row is inserted into a table with a clustered index, it must be physically placed in sorted order within the table's pages. In environments where *delete*s and *insert*s are frequent, such as many real-time transaction-processing applications, and where the primary key is a sequentially generated surrogate key, avoid the clustered index on the sequential primary key if you can. Instead, you, consider one of your candidate keys which would guarantee scattered data page accesses for both the *insert*s and the *update*s.

For duplicate, nonunique keys, a clustered index reduces I/Os for retrievals, since duplicate rows are more likely to be either on the same page or sequentially adjoining pages. This is not the case with either nonclustered indexes or tables with no index at all, where each duplicate-key row could be physically far removed from other duplicate rows within the table.

For some columns and tables that may seem to meet most of the criteria for applying a clustered index, this still may not be a wise choice. An index with low selectivity may not be the most effective use of the clustered index, no matter how many times the indexed column appears in a search or join clause. For example, a "gender" column with only two possible values (male and female) is not a good candidate for your index. When building indexes, either clustered or nonclustered, look for columns whose values result in high selectivity—columns with the most unique values.

**Note**

When specifying a composite index, always specify the column with the most unique values first. SQL Server only stores index statistics on the first column of a composite index.

Tables with very few rows (tables with less than 3 to 5 data pages total), or tables whose rows are rarely selected before being either updated or deleted, may not be good candidates for a clustered index.

Similarly, if a table has very large rows in which most of the columns are rarely accessed, and one or two columns are frequently accessed, use a nonclustered index instead to support index coverage of the query, as explained in the next section.

## ⑥ *Selecting a Column (or Columns) for a Nonclustered Index*

Most of the rules applied to selecting columns for the clustered index can also be used in making choices for the nonclustered index. In many systems where the primary-key column received the clustered index, typically any foreign-key columns in a table are prime candidates for a nonclustered index.

When you apply the nonclustered index, a B-Tree of pointers is maintained for the column values in a sorted order, even though the data rows themselves are not physically ordered according to the column values. This B-Tree must therefore carry more pointer information than the clustered-index B-Tree mentioned earlier. Therefore, any query requesting information about the existence of a row, may be resolved simply by a two- or three-page traversal of the nonclustered index's B-Tree, without ever accessing the table's data pages. This is called index covering, and is one of the primary benefits of a nonclustered index.

Since, for each row in the table, the indexed columns' data values are compactly stored within the B-Tree of the nonclustered index, index covering can also satisfy any query requesting data values for the indexed columns only; no access to the associated data page or pages is necessary. Therefore, the nonclustered index can provide both simple existence information as well as actual data values.

To promote index covering, evaluate the potential columns for indexing which remain after building the one clustered index. Consider combining columns into one nonclustered index versus multiple nonclustered indexes since each nonclustered index created holds at least one row for every row in the data pages of the table. When combining columns in this fashion, be mindful of ordering of the columns with respect to the most frequent versus least frequent ordering of the columns in queries. If your index places an often-sought column at the end of the index definition, the optimizer may not use your index to improve your performance.

# Epilogue

*The following list summarizes the tasks performed as you specified indexes to improve data access performance, to enforce uniqueness, or to control data distribution.*

❶ Reviewed major indexing issues.

❷ From a list of critical transactions, identified the individual tables and columns affected or used by the transactions.

❸ Selected columns that are candidates for indexes.

❹ Assessed the *update* patterns against the tables.

❺ Specified a column (or columns) for the clustered index.

❻ Specified a column (or columns) for the nonclustered indexes.

## *Some things to remember:*

► Index fitness is based more on your application query patterns than on your table definitions. The table definitions merely provide you with some hints about expected queries.

► Remember that transaction analysis should indicate the priority of speedy sequential inserts versus speedy retrieval. Typically, you'll discover that any page contention issue is trivial in comparison to the gains you receive in ordering your data and in effective use of page caching.

► In environments where *delete*s and *insert*s are frequent, such as many real-time transaction-processing applications, you may want to avoid the clustered index since it requires maintenance of both the data pages and the index pages.

▶ An index with low selectivity will never be used by the optimizer, no matter how many times the indexed column appears in a search or join clause.

▶ Similarly, the optimizer will not use a clustered index which has been applied to a table with very few rows.

▶ Be careful and efficient in creating nonclustered indexes. To ensure that such indexes will often be beneficial to the optimizer's query plan, place the most-selected column first in the order of columns comprising an index. Rank any other columns you used in the index creation according to their usefulness and then place them left to right after this column within the *create index* statement.

▶ Use the *fillfactor* configuration value to set a limit on how densely data pages and index pages can be packed while the index is being built. (Once the index is built, this value does not affect data placement.)

# Chapter 14
## *Maintaining Row Uniqueness*

## Prologue

*In this chapter, you will specify how to maintain uniqueness of primary-key values.*

> **Must you do this activity? Why or when?**
> Yes; required for data integrity.
>
> **What do you need before you start? How or where do you get it?**
> * Complete table and column definitions.
> * Primary-key definitions.
>
> **What are the tasks in this activity?**
> ① Identify the primary key of each table.
> ② Identify any other columns which may require uniqueness.
> ③ Decide on the mechanism to maintain uniqueness of primary key and other key values.

## Tasks

*Read through all the tasks in this section before you begin the first task. Perform tasks sequentially, as presented.*

### ① *Identifying the Primary Key*

The primary key value is the field, or combination of fields, that uniquely identify each row in the table. It is based on the primary-key attribute(s) identified in the logical design. In the physical design, however, you may define a surrogate key to represent the logical primary key. You must then guarantee the uniqueness of this surrogate key.

## ② *Identifying Other Columns Requiring Uniqueness*

In some data models, more than one unique value may be associated with a row, though only one of those values is declared to be the primary key value. For instance, in an accounting data model, you may track a unique order number which is generated by the buyer as well as a unique order number which is generated by the supplier as well as a unique order number which is generated by the shipper. All of these numbers represent the same row of data; each must be unique, and yet your logical model may use only one number as the primary key.

When you choose to designate a surrogate key to represent a bulky primary key, you must maintain uniqueness for the surrogate as well as for the non-primary-key composite fields.

## ③ *Maintaining Uniqueness of Primary-Key Values*

Once you have identified the primary key for a table and have identified other columns which may require uniqueness, you must decide whether to enforce their uniqueness through the use of an index, or through a trigger, or through application constraints.

### Indexes

When you create an index in SQL Server, you can choose whether or not the index allows duplicate key values. A unique index ensures that in response to an *insert* or *update* operation, no two records will have the same values within the indexed columns.

An index's ability to enforce uniqueness is particularly useful when the key values for the index represent the primary key of the data in the table. Decide which uniqueness values will be controlled via a clustered index and which will be controlled via a nonclustered index. Typically the primary key receives the clustered index, though not necessarily, as in the case of a surrogate sequential primary key (described below in "Triggers").

SQL Server 10.x provides additional unique/primary key constraints which may be used to set up your indexes. In the *create table* syntax, you can specify either *unique* or *primary key* for a column or columns in the table. Either syntax constrains the values in the indicated column or columns so that no two rows can have the same value. The *unique* keyword creates a unique nonclustered index by default; the *primary key* keyword creates a unique clustered index by default. Consult SQL Server 10.x's accompanying documentation for further details.

## Triggers

Sometimes, you may wish to implement a trigger to support uniqueness of rows, particularly if you have defined a surrogate key to represent the actual composite primary key. By using an *insert* trigger to generate unique surrogate key values and then using a unique nonclustered index on the surrogate to control *insert and update* activities, you can ensure your surrogate uniquely identifies each row in your table.

 **WARNING!**
Do not use the clustered index to enforce uniqueness on surrogate sequential keys; this creates a grave performance impact. Use a unique nonclustered index instead.

You may also choose trigger-controlled uniqueness if you do not wish to take up room in your database with the index pages which accompany index-controlled uniqueness. Choose this option if your table is less than 5 pages long, and if you seldom retrieve your rows based on the field in which you are maintaining uniqueness.

## Application code

Finally, you can always choose to provide all of the aforementioned functionality at the application level. Though this is rarely recommended, you may find this option necessary. For instance, if you must maintain uniqueness in conjunction with another set of data not in SQL Server, then your application code will have to provide the functions normally provided through the indexes.

# Epilogue

*The following list summarizes the tasks performed as you specified how to maintain uniqueness of primary-key values.*

❶ Identified the primary key of each table.
❷ Identified any other columns which may require uniqueness.

❸ Decided on the mechanism to maintain uniqueness of primary key and other key values:
- using indexes
- using triggers
- handling uniqueness in the application code

## *Some things to remember:*

▶ If you choose to use the SQL Server 10.x *unique* syntax to enforce uniqueness, be aware that it creates a unique nonclustered index by default. Similarly, the *primary key* syntax creates a unique clustered index by default.

▶ Do not use the clustered index to enforce uniqueness on surrogate sequential keys; this creates a grave performance impact. Use a unique nonclustered index instead.

# Chapter 15
# *Handling Domain Restrictions*

## Prologue_____

*In this chapter, you will specify a set of acceptable values for a particular data element (domain). This typically entails defining SQL Server rules and defaults on the columns of a table, to maintain valid data values within the columns.*

**Must you do this activity? Why or when?**
Yes; required for data integrity.

**What do you need before you start? How or where do you get it?**
- Complete table and column definitions.
- Naming conventions.
- Domain-restriction specification from logical design.

**What are the tasks in this activity?**
① Identify columns that have domain restrictions.
② Consider using a SQL Server rule on a column, to guarantee that the column's value falls within a domain.
③ Consider using a SQL Server default on a column, to populate it when inserting rows into the table.
④ Consider the use of the *default* and *constraint* features of SQL Server 10.x *create table* syntax.

## *Some things to keep in mind*

■ Certain domain restrictions are too complex for SQL Server rules and defaults to handle; enforce them by other means such as a trigger or stored procedure.

# Tasks

*Read through all the tasks in this section before you begin the first task. Perform tasks sequentially, as presented.*

## ① *Identifying Columns that Have Domain Restrictions*

Simply stated, a domain is the set of all acceptable data values for a particular attribute of a database object. Every column has a domain. SQL Server uses datatypes to enforce simple domains. However, certain types of domain restrictions cannot be enforced solely through datatypes. For example, the column ne_state must contain a state abbreviation for one of the New England states. The datatype for this column is *char(2)*. Another example is emp_age, which must be a number between 18 and 65. The datatype for this column is *tinyint*.

For more complex domain restrictions, consider the use of triggers, views, stored procedures, and application code as discussed in Chapter 18, "Handling Complex Integrity Constraints."

## ② *Using SQL Server Rules*

With SQL Server, you can quickly restrict domains by using rules. Once you have defined a rule, you can apply it to any attribute whose domain is correctly limited by the rule.

When using rules:

- Identify a rule for every primary key in your schema.
- Apply a primary key's rule to every instance of a foreign key to that primary key.
- Be as specific as possible when identifying an attribute's domain.

A quick and efficient way to enforce rules over many primary-key and foreign-key columns is to bind the rule to a user-defined datatype used for those columns.

## ③ *Using SQL Server Defaults*

Consider an appropriate default value for every column that sports a rule. Designate a default that is within the domain restrictions of the rule and is a viable non-null value to fill the column when the user does not provide a value.

## ④ *SQL Server 10.x* Default *and* Constraint Checks

In SQL Server 10.x, additional features exist to define and restrict the data domain within a table. These are the *default* feature and the *check* feature which provide domain restriction language within the *create table* syntax. Through this construct, the notion of domain is now integrally linked with the relational notion.

These new constraints limit the values that can be inserted into the table much as pre-SQL Server 10.x *defaults* and *rules* did. You can still use the *create rule* and *create default* syntax if you wish, however the advantage of the new constraints is that they are not separate database objects to be maintained. Furthermore, when you need to redefine domain restrictions, you can do so through the *default* and *constraint* constructs in the *alter table* syntax.

Remember the advantages of the pre-10.x constructs *create rule* and *create default*. They allow you to apply rules and defaults to either columns or datatypes. Moreover, you can define rules and defaults once and then bind them to many different objects without having to redefine them each time.

# Epilogue

*The following list summarizes the tasks performed as you specified a set of acceptable values for a particular data element (domain).*

❶ Identified columns that have domain restrictions.

❷ Considered using a SQL Server rule on a column, to guarantee that the column's value falls within a domain.

❸ Considered using a SQL Server default on a column, to populate it when inserting rows into the table.

❹ Considered the use of the *default* and *check* features of SQL Server 10.x *create table* syntax.

# Chapter 16
## *Handling Referential Integrity*

## Prologue_____

*In this chapter, you will decide how to handle:*

- *primary-key update and delete constraints*
- *foreign-key insert, update, and delete constraints using either SQL Server triggers or SQL Server 10.x declarative-integrity constructs.*

**Must you do this activity? Why or when?**

Yes; required for data integrity.

**What do you need before you start? How or where do you get it?**

- Complete table and column definitions.
- Referential-integrity document from logical design.

**What are the tasks in this activity?**

① Identify primary key/foreign key relationships.
② Set bounds for referential-integrity constraints.
③ Decide on primary-key *update* and *delete* constraints.
④ Decide on foreign-key *insert* and *update* constraints.
⑤ Decide on foreign-key *delete* constraints.
⑥ Based on the identified constraints, decide on the applicability of declarative integrity in SQL Server 10.x.

## Tasks_____

*Read through all the tasks in this section before you begin the first task. Perform tasks sequentially, as presented.*

## ① *Identifying Primary-Key/Foreign-Key Relationships*

The relational model relies on the primary key/foreign key construct to explicitly relate values in one table with values in another table.

A foreign key, therefore, refers to the primary key of another table. A referential-integrity design constrains how foreign keys will behave in response to a change in the table containing that key as a primary key. Similarly, such a design restricts changes to the foreign key, enforcing a continued relationship with the foreign key.

Strict referential-integrity designs guarantee that all foreign keys in a relational database must either be null or contain a value belonging to an associated primary-key table.

## ② *Setting the Bounds for Referential-Integrity Constraints*

The goals of referential-integrity design are to:
- preserve data relationships: all *insert*, *update*, and *delete* actions performed against a database must result in foreign-key values that are null or that match associated primary keys
- minimize coding of enforcement within each application that will use the database
- contribute to overall data integrity

Referential-integrity design *does not* include design considerations for:
- uniqueness—this is an entity integrity issue
- data formatting
- enforcing correct column datatypes and lengths
- nulls in nonkey data
- default values in nonkey data

SYBASE SQL Server provides extensive support for maintaining referential integrity. Triggers are implemented to control every aspect of the *insert/ update/delete* cycle. Additionally, declarative referential integrity has been added to SQL Server 10.x through *primary key/foreign key* constraints and through *check* constraints.

## ③ *Deciding on Primary-Key* Update *and* Delete *Constraints*

For each table in your database, decide how the primary-key value will affect foreign-key values in *update* and *delete* operations. You may choose:
- restricted

- cascaded to all tables containing that key as a foreign key
- allowed, and all matching foreign-key values will be set to null
- allowed, and all matching foreign-key values will be set to a default value
- allowed, with no effect on matching foreign-key values

## Restrictive constraints

Restrictive constraints provide the highest level of data integrity. No changes are allowed to the primary key.

You cannot delete the primary-key value as long as there are any matching foreign keys. You must first modify the data to change or delete all matching-key information.

Primary-key *update* statements are usually restricted for:

- data that has complex relationships with other data, since a single change to a primary key might affect a large percentage of system data
- data that has been transferred out of the system; for instance, by archiving

Primary-key *delete* statements are typically restricted in the following situations:

- Critical detail or child information; see Figure 16.1

**Figure 16.1 Primary-key delete constraints example**-----------------------------------

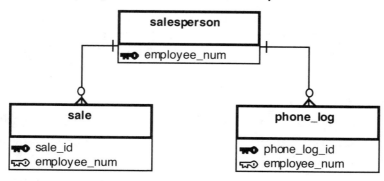

*The salesperson/sale relationship defined previously is too critical to allow for cascading deletions of a single salesperson row. Require deletion of all sales information related to a salesperson before allowing the salesperson to be deleted.*

*Salesperson/phone_log does not share the critical nature of the salesperson/sale relationship. There is no apparent reason to restrict deletions based on the existence of phone_log records.*

- Data is updated from more than one location; see Figure 16.2 for an example.

Figure 16.2 Primary-key delete constraints example---------------------------------

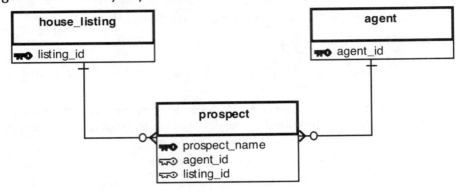

The prospect table in Figure 16.2 could be updated from a dozen competing real estate offices in the same organization. The decision to delete a house_listing for any reason other than a sale would not be allowed as long as a single prospect for the listing still existed.

Therefore, the designer restricts the deletion of house_listing to protect the existence of prospects.

## Cascading constraints

You can enforce referential integrity through cascading *delete*s or cascading *update*s.

When a primary key is deleted, all rows containing matching foreign keys are also automatically deleted. A cascading constraint is riskier than a restrictive one. *Delete*s automatically trigger *delete*s, which in turn can trigger other *delete*s. Cascading primary-key *update*s enable the user to change large amounts of data with a single *update*.

Primary-key *update*s are usually cascaded for:

- name-based key systems like personnel systems or licensing systems
- status/availability systems such as reservations/ticketing systems
- scheduling systems

Primary-key *delete*s are typically cascaded in the following situations (see Figure 16.3):

- Data that goes in as a unit gets deleted as a unit.
- Nonpermanent data: volatile rows of foreign-key data are usually candidates for cascading deletion. See Figure 16.4.

**100**

Figure 16.3 Primary-key deleting cascade example --------------------------------

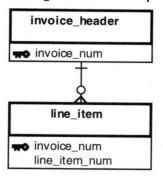

*An invoice_header is created with one or more line_item rows. Parent and child rows are created simultaneously. Deleting an invoice_header (primary key) should cascade out and delete all line_item (foreign-key) rows.*

Figure 16.4 Foreign-key deleting cascade example ----------------------------------

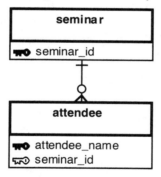

*In a convention tracking system, seminars are frequently added, deleted, and changed. The developer designs the seminar/attendees relationship to allow cascading deletes of all attendees (no seminar/ no attendees).*

 **Note**
Restrictive and cascading constraints are the most commonly used referential-integrity techniques.

## Nullifying constraints

When a primary key is updated or deleted all matching foreign keys are set to null. A nullifying-key *update* works only in situations where null is allowed in the foreign-key column. A nullifying-key *delete* works only in situations where null foreign keys are acceptable.

 **WARNING !**
Careless use of a nullifying constraint can leave gaping holes in a database, where data can't be found or a matching relationship can't be made.

## Defaulting constraints

When a primary key is updated or deleted, all matching foreign keys are set to a default value. This method can be fairly effective if you ensure that the default value always has a corresponding record in the primary-key database.

Nullifying/defaulting primary key *delete*s are used more often than their *update* counterparts. Default-value key *delete*s require the existence of a row with the default value as its primary key.

Nullifying or defaulting a foreign key when its primary key is deleted is usually reserved for primary-key data that is time dependent. Time constraints imply that foreign-key data need not be strictly associated with primary-key values. Once a primary key changes, its foreign keys are simply rendered irrelevant.

Primary-key *update*s are usually nullified/defaulted for optional lookup data.

Primary-key *delete*s are typically nullified/defaulted in the following situations:

- time-sensitive lookup data
- optional lookup data

## No constraints

Some designers place no referential-integrity constraints on a database. Avoid this option since it forces the application to maintain integrity.

## ④ *Deciding on Foreign-Key* Insert *and* Update *Constraints*

For each table containing a foreign key in your database, decide how to handle the foreign-key value in *insert* and *update* operations. You may choose to:

- restrict operations on foreign keys.
- automatically add a new primary-key value.
- nullify foreign-key values.
- set foreign-key defaults.
- do nothing to foreign keys.

## Restrictive constraints

No foreign-key value can be inserted or updated if no corresponding primary-key value exists in the associated table. This is a typical means of enforcing referential integrity for most foreign-key situations, especially those dealing with lookup tables. Such a restrictive form comprises the vast majority of all foreign-key constraints.

A restricted foreign-key *insert/update* constraint enforces foreign key validation; foreign-key values are validated against a primary-key entity before the data action is accepted.

Restrictive constraint is typically used in the following situations:

- Lookup attributes must have related primary keys (see Figure 16.5).

**Figure 16.5 Lookup attributes example** --------------------------------------------------

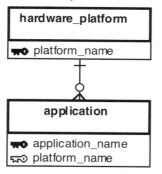

*The application table has a foreign key that "looks up" into the hardware_platform table. An application must have a hardware platform that exists as a primary key in the hardware_platform table.*

- Subtype data cannot exist without associated supertype rows (see Figure 16.6).
- There can be no child rows without the presence of a parent row with the same key value (see Figure 16.7).

## Automatic constraints

If the user or application adds a foreign-key value that does not match a primary key in the associated table, update the primary table with a row containing the foreign-key value as its primary key. Although this enforcement of referential integrity is used less often than restricted *insert/update*, it is extremely useful when a foreign-key table is the main entry point into a data system and the users do not wish to have to update the primary-key table every time they introduce a new record type.

Figure 16.6 Supertype/subtype example -----------------------------------------------

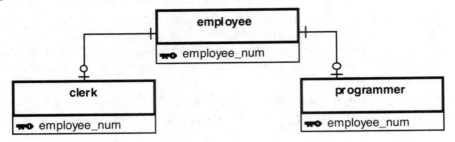

Figure 16.7 Parent/child example ----------------------------------------------------------

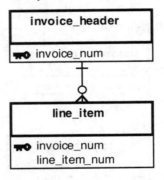

*No line_item can exist without an associated invoice_header row.*

This constraint is typically used in the following situations:

- Users add foreign-key values that do not have associated primary key rows.

- Users insert rows into the parent or super table with the associated foreign key as the skeletal-row value. Skeletal rows are primary-key table rows that contain only primary-key information.

For example, see Figure 16.8.

## Nullifying constraints

New foreign keys are set to null when a row is inserted and the foreign-key value has no match in the primary-key table.

Null/defaulting constraints make up most foreign-key control not handled by *restrictive* constraints.

## Figure 16.8 Automatic constraints example ------------------------------------------

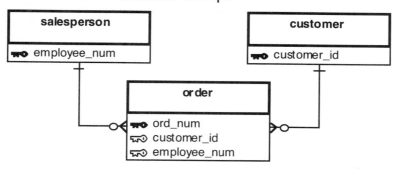

*Where these business rules apply:*

* *Most data entry is performed by the entry clerks at the point of sale.*

* *Data-entry clerks are responsible only for logging incoming orders.*

* *To minimize entry times (and thus customer waiting periods), a clerk may enter an order that has no associated customer.*

* *The new customer is automatically entered into the customer table.*

* *The salesperson record must exist before order entry is possible.*

* *Orders use restrictive constraints for salesperson foreign-key inserts/updates and automatic constraints for customer foreign-key updates.*

* *If the ordering customer does not exist, a skeletal record is automatically inserted into the customer table. The account manager is responsible for filling out the customer record at some future time.*

 **Note**

Nullifying and defaulting constraints apply only to inserts—not updates—of a foreign key.

Nullifying values are used in situations where foreign-key data is not required and is unknown during row inserts. See Figure 16.9 for an example.

## Defaulting constraints

New foreign keys are set to a default value when a row is inserted and the foreign-key value has no match in the primary-key table.

Default values are used in situations where foreign keys almost always fall into a single class, or where a row specifying "unknown value" resides in the primary-key table. (See Figure 16.10.)

## Figure 16.9 Nullifying constraints example --------------------------------------------

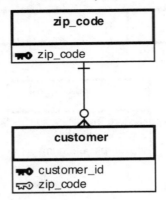

*Where the business rule for the above data relationship is:*

• *If the address portion of the customer data sheet is blank, the zip code is unknown.*

## Figure 16.10 Defaulting constraints example --------------------------------------------

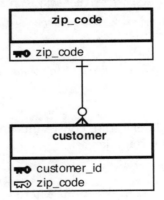

*Where the business rule for the above data relationship is:*

• *If the address portion of the customer data sheet is blank, the default zip code is assumed.*

**Note**

You can use default values when you estimate an attribute's value. If 95% of employees are assigned to a single department, you can reasonably guess that a new employee will be so assigned.

## No Constraints

Some designers provide no referential integrity constraints. *Avoid this option.*

# ⑤ *Foreign-Key Deletes*

Foreign-key deletions rarely carry any restrictions because foreign-key rows do not affect tables below them. You do have to be aware of rows containing foreign keys and also containing primary keys used as foreign keys in associated tables. Such instances may require a cascading *delete* of all associated foreign-key values, as described earlier in "Primary Key *Update* and *Delete* Constraints."

# ⑥ *Declarative Referential Integrity*

The Integrity Enhancement feature in SQL Server 10.x lets you specify referential integrity constraints in the *create table* statement, using the *references* construct. These constraints ensure that a primary key exists in another table if you are inserting or updating a foreign key table. (This is an automatic *restrictive* constraint.)

Note that declarative referential integrity lets you design a *restrictive* constraint on foreign-key *insert*s and *update*s. You must use triggers to implement any other referential integrity constraint on primary-key *update*s and *delete*s or foreign key *update*s and *insert*s.

# Epilogue

*The following list summarizes the tasks performed as you decided how to handle referential integrity.*

❶ Identified primary key/foreign key relationships.

❷ Set bounds for referential integrity constraints.

❸ Decided on primary-key *update* and *delete* constraints. For each table, decided whether the primary-key value on *delete* or *update* would be:

- restricted

- cascaded to all tables containing that key as a foreign key

- allowed, and all matching foreign-key values will be set to null

- allowed, and all matching foreign-key values will be set to a default value
- allowed, with no effect on matching foreign-key values

❹ Decided on foreign-key *insert* and *update* constraints. For each table containing a foreign key, decided if the foreign-key value on *insert* or *update* would be:

- restricted
- allowed, and a new row added to the table containing the primary key
- set to null
- set to a default value
- allowed, with no reference to the primary key

❺ Decided on foreign-key *delete* constraints.

❻ Based on the identified constraints, decided on the applicability of declarative integrity in SQL Server 10.x.

## Some things to remember:

▶ If you choose a nullifying constraint on foreign keys when the matching primary key is updated or delete, you may end up with many holes in your database.

▶ Consider a default foreign-key constraint for primary-key *update* and *delete* integrity when the primary-key data is time dependent; that is, due to time constraints, the foreign-key values need not be strictly associated with primary-key values. Once a primary key is changed, its foreign keys are simply rendered irrelevant.

▶ Also consider a default value for a foreign-key *insert* constraint when you can consistently estimate an attribute's value for the majority of cases.

▶ Do not consider default or nullifying constraints when performing an *update* of a foreign key.

# Chapter 17

# *Maintaining Derived and Redundant Data*

## Prologue_____

*In this chapter, you will specify how to maintain data integrity if the data model contains derived and/or redundant data.*

**Must you do this activity? Why or when?**

Only if you have added derived or redundant data to the tables in previous activities.

**What do you need before you start? How or where do you get it?**

- The output of all previous denormalization activities in which you added derived or redundant data (Chapters 4, 5, 9, and 10).

- Complete table and column definitions.

- Primary-key definitions.

**What are the tasks in this activity?**

① Identify derived and/or redundant data.

② Decide on a mechanism to maintain derived and/or redundant data.

## Tasks_____

*Read through all the tasks in this section before you begin the first task. Perform tasks sequentially, as presented.*

## ① *Identifying Derived and/or Redundant Data*

You may have added derived and redundant data to the database in these earlier chapters:

Chapter 4, "Adding Redundant Columns"

Chapter 5, "Adding Derived Columns"

Chapter 9, "Duplicating Parts of Tables"

Chapter 10, "Adding Tables for Derived Data"

Remember that you must always maintain derived or redundant data. That is, you must ensure integrity between the source data and the derived or redundant data.

When deciding whether to use derived or redundant data, you must consider the volatility of the source columns and rows. If the source information is constantly being updated, you may incur severe performance penalties in maintaining integrity between the primary data and its copies.

## ② *Mechanisms to Maintain Derived or Redundant Data*

When you are determining what mechanisms to use in maintaining the derived or redundant data in your database, consider using:

- triggers
- other application logic
- Open Server logic

### Using triggers

SQL Server triggers are commonly used to maintain derived or redundant data. Updating the source data fires a trigger automatically to update any data based on the source data.

For example, you can use a trigger in the sample database, pubs, to update the total_sales column in the titles table each time a new sales order is added.

The example Figure 4.1 used in Chapter 4 includes the redundant column pubname in the titles table. This column can be kept current by using a trigger. The trigger will fire whenever the publishers table is updated. If pubname is changed in the publishers table, the trigger will make the same change in the titles table.

Always use triggers to maintain redundant data. Use triggers to maintain derived data when the calculation is not too complex and relies strictly on data available within the database.

## Using other application logic

You can also maintain derived data in your database by embedding the maintenance code in your application.

Avoid this method if possible. It can expose your data to integrity problems. For example, if multiple applications (which do not share the same code) update the same source data, they may not create/update the derived data consistently. Data integrity may also be compromised if users update the source data directly, instead of using the application.

However, if your derived columns rely on data not available in the database, or if your columns' values are the result of algorithms too complex to express in SQL, use your application logic to derive the values.

Be forewarned! In such situations, your data's integrity is extremely vulnerable to a potential lack of synchronization and unintended, costly duplication of effort in maintaining the data. Avoid such application-dependent columns when possible.

## Using Open Server application logic

Finally, you might consider executing a remote procedure call (RPC) in a trigger to an Open Server application. This technique combines the two other ways of supporting derived and redundant data. It has both the rigor of the trigger and the flexibility of the application code.

# Epilogue

*The following list summarizes the tasks performed as you specified how to maintain data integrity if the data model contained derived and/or redundant data.*

❶ Identified derived and/or redundant data.
❷ Decided on a mechanism to maintain derived and/or redundant data:
  • using triggers
  • using other application logic
  • using Open Server logic

## *Some things to remember:*

▶ Always use triggers to maintain redundant data.

▶ Use triggers to maintain derived data when the calculation is not too complex and relies strictly on data available within the database.

▶ If you must use application logic to maintain derived data, your data's integrity is extremely at risk, vulnerable to synchronization problems. In addition, you may be adding unintended and costly duplication of effort in maintaining the data.

# Chapter 18

## *Handling Complex Integrity Constraints*

## Prologue_____

*In this chapter, you will decide how to handle complex business rules such as sequence rules, cross-domain business rules, and complex data-domain rules.*

> **Must you do this activity? Why or when?**
>
> Yes; required for data integrity.
>
> **What do you need before you start? How or where do you get it?**
>
> • Complete column and table definitions.
>
> • Business-rules specification from requirements-specification document and logical design.
>
> **What are the tasks in this activity?**
>
> ① Identify columns constrained by complex business rules that SQL Server *rules*, *defaults*, or *constraints* do not handle.
>
> ② Decide which technique to use to enforce complex rules.

## Tasks_____

*Read through all the tasks in this section before you begin the first task. Perform tasks sequentially, as presented.*

## ① *Identifying Columns Constrained by Complex Business Rules*

SQL Server datatypes, defaults, rules, and constraints are used to enforce a column's domain and associated restrictions. However, data values in certain columns are restricted by business rules that cannot be enforced using these mechanisms.

For example:

- The allowed data value in one column depends on the value in another column.
- The new data value in a column depends on the previous value.
- The domain contains a nonfinite set of values.

## ② *Deciding How to Handle Complex Business Rules*

When you decide how to implement and maintain complex business rules, base your decision on the type of business rule you need to support:

- sequence
- cross-domain
- mutually exclusive
- mutually inclusive
- data-dependent
- complex domains

Once you have identified any complex business rules in your system, you must determine the most appropriate technique to enforce those rules. The choices are:

- triggers
- views
- remote procedure calls to an external application
- local application code

You must decide based on the specific type of rule you wish to enforce. SQL Server normally uses triggers to implement complex business rules.

### Sequence rules

In some systems, certain steps must be done in a particular order. Sequence rules define the order of these steps. You can use triggers to enforce the proper sequence of these steps.

Manufacturing processes, and many other systems, have a sequencing requirement. In many cases, a status or indicator value must change from one value to another in a prescribed sequence.

For example, a personnel system goes through the following steps to hire a new employee:

1. Open a personnel requisition.

2. Make offer.

3. Offer accepted.

4. Employee starts—requisition filled.

The requisition status starts as "open" and must proceed sequentially through "offered," "accepted," and "filled." Each step must be performed in sequence. A trigger can ensure that this occurs.

## Cross-domain (intra-row) business rules

Some business rules may constrain relationships between two or more columns in a table. Intra-row business rules or cross-domain integrity rules specify what combinations of values in these columns are valid. You can use triggers to enforce these types of rules. The following cases are examined next:

- mutually exclusive rules
- mutually inclusive rules
- data-dependent values.

Examples are based on the employee entity shown in Figure 18.1.

Figure 18.1 Employee table example -------------------------------------------------------

| employee |
|---|
| 🔑 employee_num |
| employee_num<br>name<br>hire_date<br>termination_date<br>annual_salary<br>hourly_wage<br>dependent_life_insurance<br>dependent_life_insurance_amount |

## Mutually exclusive rules

If a given row has a value in column A, a mutually exclusive rule can specify that there must be no value for that row in column B, and vice versa. The two columns are mutually exclusive. For example, an employee is either a salaried employee or an hourly employee. If the employee is salaried, then the record must hold a value for annual_salary, and none for hourly_wage. If the employee is hourly, then the record must contain a value for hourly_wage, and none for annual_salary.

You can create an *insert/update* trigger to enforce this business rule. Your trigger must prevent the insertion of a row that has non-null values in both the annual_salary and the hourly_wage columns. Also, when the row is updated, the trigger must verify that only one of those columns contains a non-null value.

In addition, in SQL Server 10.x, you can create a view with the *with check option* syntax which imposes a view integrity over the data. All data modification statements are validated against the view selection criteria; all rows inserted or updated through the view must remain visible through the view.

## Mutually inclusive rules

Mutually inclusive rules specify that, for a given row, if a value is present in column A, there must be a value in column B. For example, if an employee elects dependent_life_insurance coverage, the dependent_life_insurance_amount column must also hold a value. The dependent_life_insurance column is mutually inclusive with the dependent_life_insurance_amount column.

You can create an *insert/update* trigger to enforce this business rule. Your trigger should prevent the insertion of a row that contains a non-null value for only one of the columns. Also, when the row is updated, the trigger must verify that both columns contain non-null values or both columns are null.

As stated earlier for mutually exclusive rules, you can create a view with the *with check option* syntax which imposes a view integrity over the data. The *select* statement of the view can contain a *where* clause which enforces this inclusion rule.

## Data-dependent values

Other business rules may specify that if the value in column A is "X," then the value in column B must be "Y." The value contained in one column is dependent on the value in another column or columns. For example, the termination_date entered for an employee must be greater than or equal to that employee's hire_date.

You can create an *update* trigger to enforce this business rule. When the employee's termination_date is updated, the trigger prevents the *update* if the termination_date predates the hire_date.

## Complex domains

SQL Server rules can check editing of values inserted into the database. However, some columns have values with very complex domains which make rule definition quite difficult. Many encoded attributes have complex domains: insurance policy numbers, bank account numbers, vehicle identification numbers, social security numbers, etc. Although you should avoid using encoded attributes, you may need them.

For example:

*An insurance policy number consists of the following parts:*

- *insurance type (automobile, life, homeowners): one character*
- *region issuing policy: one-digit integer*
- *policy year: two-digit integer*
- *policy serial number: six-digit integer*
- *check digit: one-digit integer*

*You can create a rule to validate the format of the insurance policy number. But no rule can validate the policy number. The second character of the policy number may be numeric, but it may not be a valid region number. Also, the calculation to generate the check digit is too complicated to be performed in a rule.*

*You could write an insert/update trigger to check that each part of the policy number is valid. When the user inserts or updates a policy number, the trigger can check that the issuing region exists in another table. It can also calculate the appropriate check digit and compare it with the check digit entered.*

For complex domain definitions, consider using a trigger that accesses current domain-restriction data within a table you maintain specifically for that purpose. Such a mechanism provides flexibility in restriction in these ways:

- You can define restrictions as dependent on the existence (or nonexistence) of other data elements within your database.

- Restrictions can have a temporal sense; that is, you can set a starting date and an expiration date for certain domain classifications.

- Users can have their own restrictions, used only for their personal data. Such a scheme can support the notion of "candidate data," where a less experienced analyst's entries are not allowed entered into the target table, but go instead to a holding table for review by a supervisor.

- You can change the data defining the domain restrictions used by the trigger without having to redefine the trigger. Changing data values in a rule or a check constraint requires redefinition of the rule or constraint.

Once again, consider the use of the SQL Server 10.x *create view* command and its *with check option* syntax to enforce these complex rules through the *where* clause selection criteria.

# Epilogue

*The following list summarizes the tasks performed as you decided how to handle complex business rules such as sequence rules, cross-domain business rules, and complex data-domain rules.*

❶ Identified columns constrained by complex business rules that SQL Server rules and defaults do not handle.

❷ Decided which technique to use to enforce complex rules. Based your decision on the type of business rule you need to support:
  - sequence
  - cross-domain
  - mutually exclusive
  - mutually inclusive
  - data-dependent
  - complex domains

## *Some things to remember:*

▶ Consider using a trigger to enforce sequence rules.

▶ You can use the check constraint to enforce mutually inclusive and mutually exclusive rules.

▶ An update trigger is useful for enforcing data-dependent values.

▶ For complex domain definitions, consider using a trigger that accesses current domain-restriction data within another table you maintain specifically for that purpose. Such a mechanism allows you to change the data defining the domain without having to redefine the logic that uses it.

# Chapter 19
## *Controlling Access to Data*

## Prologue

*In this chapter, you will restrict access to commands and data.*

**Must you do this activity? Why or when?**

Yes, if security is a concern.

**What do you need before you start? How or where do you get it?**

- Complete column and table definitions.
- Security specifications from logical design.

**What are the tasks in this activity?**

① Understand access and security issues.

② Decide who will have system-administration and database- owner privileges.

③ Decide user and group permissions.

④ Consider using stored procedures to restrict access to data.

⑤ Consider using views to restrict access to data.

⑥ Consider using Sybase Secure SQL Server.

⑦ Consider using multiple databases.

⑧ Consider using SQL Server 10.x security features.

## Tasks

*Read through all the tasks in this section before you begin the first task. Perform tasks sequentially, as presented.*

# ① *Understanding Access and Security Issues*

As you develop a physical design for your database, you must address the twin issues of data access and data security. With respect to both your development staff and the end-user community, you must decide how sensitive your data is, what sorts of operations to allow on what data, and whom you allow to perform these operations.

Certainly, you could enforce perfect integrity of your data by denying everyone access to it. But if one intent of your database is to promote data sharing, then restricting access conflicts with your data-sharing goals. Your design must strike a balance between optimal protection and optimal sharing of the data.

You can strike that balance by answering these questions:

- Who will evaluate the sensitivity of data in the database?
- How will you distribute designated security roles in the organization?
- For each intended user of the database, what is the minimum necessary set of accesses and functions?
- Under what procedures will these users do their work?
- Which people and which actions should you track for their impact on data integrity?

# ② *Assigning System Administration and DBO Privileges*

In the 4.x versions of SQL Server, only one *login* has access to all objects within the server and all functions supported by the server. That is the *sa* (for system administrator) account. Whoever has the *sa* account password can execute all commands and access all data. Users using the *sa* login need not identify themselves by any other user account name.

In SQL Server 10.x, this login still exists. However, the full set of capabilities has additionally been divided among three *roles*, which can be assigned to any login:

- SA (System Administrator) includes the functions and privileges needed for all database and server administration;
- SSO (Site Security Officer) includes the functions and privileges needed for the security officer's tasks, such as granting and revoking access to database objects;
- OPER (operator) includes database backup and recovery functions, for use by an operator.

Roles are valuable in maintaining users' identities while performing critical system functions. Because a role is assigned to an existing user account, that user name is still associated with any of the actions performed in any of the three roles.

## Least privilege

You must provide security measures to protect your database, both during the development phase, and in the end-user's environment. Decide how many users (logins) need each of the three special roles. Keep in mind the notion of *least privilege*—users should have only those privileges they need to do their jobs. Try to avoid allowing any one person to take on all three roles.

The best solution is to give the SA role to the primary system administrator and then give the same role to one other person, as a backup to the primary. Then designate one primary SSO, and appoint one backup; and designate one primary OPER and appoint one backup. This plan provides that no one has total control of the database, and no one is indispensable, since each primary person has a backup; however, it does involve six persons in the overall administration of you server and databases. To reduce this number, you can appoint each of your primaries as the backup for one of the other roles—thus involving only three people in administering your database.

In large installations, you may want to appoint a staff of OPER users (rather than just one primary and one backup) to support the demands of volume changes for backup and load procedures.

## What to do with the *sa* login

In non-SQL Server 10.x environments, guard the *sa* login closely. Grant sa access to the least possible number of users, and ensure strict protection of the account password. Try to limit the number of users who have access to the *sa* account to two; the greater the number of people who have such privileges, the greater the risk of data-integrity comprise, either accidental or malicious.

In SQL Server 10.x environments, if you have a small installation, you may consider maintaining the *sa* login as the sole means of access and accountability for system administration and security tasks. If so, limit the number of users who have access to the account. Even in SQL Server 10.x, because the login name is the identity of the user, any actions performed by an *sa* login cannot be traced back to the actual user. Encourage use of the SA role instead.

Typically, to promote accountability and the notion of "least privilege," you should lock this super-user account after having assigned each of the three roles to at least one user. (SQL Server 10.x requires at least one unlocked login that possesses the System Administrator role, and one that possesses the System Security Officer role.)

**Note**
If you decide to lock the *sa* account, be sure to check all scripts that may contain the *sa* login name and password. Scripts cannot run if they are meant to run as *sa* and that account is locked. Change the logins in those scripts to the name of a user with the correct role.

# ③ *Determining Privileges for Users and Groups of Users*

Once you have identified the hierarchy of users who need special role privileges, map out the specific privileges each of the other users needs:

- select privileges
- data-modification privileges
- privileges to execute stored procedures
- privileges to execute commands

Work with the designated SSO during your physical-design phase, since data-protection issues may make you reconsider your intended model. The SSO can help you identify the accesses that might conflict with your design.

## What access controls to use

All SQL Server products have a set of commands called Discretionary Access Control. The SA or SSO uses these commands to grant or deny a given user access to database objects and commands. Consult your *Commands Reference Manuals* and *System Administration Guide* for the complete hierarchy of these privileges and their effect on the hierarchy of database objects. SQL Server 10.x contains new permissions such as *references* which may affect the accesses of users to your database objects unknowingly. For instance, to use the *references* constraint in the *create table* syntax for a table, you must have *references* permission on the referenced table, not on the table being created.

The SQL functions are divided into identification functions, which are executed through system functions; and access-control functions, which are executed in Transact-SQL. The access-control functions include two kinds of permissions: command permissions and object permissions. The SSO uses these SQL functions first to identify users, and then to restrict each user to the minimal set of necessary database objects and commands.

As you set up identification for access control, remember:

- Provide ALL users with their own login names. Do not promote or allow sharing of logins. In SQL Server 10.x, a non-null password is required on all logins. For SQL Server 4.x releases, you must enforce the use of passwords administratively.

- When you grant a user access to a database, add that user's name to the database's access list.

- Avoid relying on the *guest* user account for access to databases. It does not let you know who has access to your data. In 4.x systems, however, be careful not to remove the *guest* privileges from master, as users may not be able to log in.

- Do not give users the *master* database as their default database.

Give these guidelines to the designated SSO and SA for subsequent enactment through scripts.

## CRUD charts

Once you have identified your set of users and applications developers, consult your database schema to determine which objects each user needs. Enumerate the commands needed with those objects. To diagram your user's needs, make a CRUD (*c*reate, *r*ead, *u*pdate, *d*elete) chart. Place all your users' names along one axis of a grid, all your database objects along the other axis of the grid. For each object listed, determine each user's set of needed accesses.

Your CRUD chart may show that sets of users share similar data needs and functional responsibilities. Therefore, you can treat them as a well-defined group of users, appointing accesses to the group as an entity rather than to each individual. (Since users can belong to only one group at a time, consider using aliases to implement a two-level hierarchical grouping.)

You can also perform this exercise on a table-by-table basis. That is, produce a CRUD chart for each table in the database; the items along the object axis are now the columns for the table.

## Access control via changes to your schema

Your analysis of user/group accesses to objects and to columns within table objects may reveal that your schema allows or requires too much unnecessary access. If so, use your CRUD charts to review your schema and change some of the relationships, subdividing some objects into multiple objects with well-defined and uniform accesses.

*For instance, you may discover that, after normalization, your schema of accounting information contains one table with some columns used by all accounts payable staff, but also some sensitive columns, such as royalty and advance, which are fairly sensitive and which should be seen only by senior accounting management. You can protect these sensitive attributes by dividing the ta-*

*ble into two tables: one to which all staff members are granted access, and one to which only management personnel are granted access.*

## ④ *Using Stored Procedures as a Security Mechanism*

A user with permission to execute a stored procedure can do so even if he or she does not have permissions on the tables or views to which the procedure refers. For example, you might give a user permission to execute a stored procedure that updates a row-and-column subset of a specified table, and not give that user any other permissions on that table.

Stored procedures are a common, effective means of protecting data integrity. To use them, however, you must address the problem of ownership chains in the design phase, to ensure that your intended security mechanisms work. As you and the SSO resolve access issues in the schema and in the intended environments, you must track ownership of each object to ensure that view and stored-procedure protections are enforced.

When a user accesses a view or a stored procedure, SQL Server does not check permissions on any of the underlying objects (other views, other procedures, tables) if the same user owns all of these objects, and if all of the underlying objects are in the same database. If the ownership chain is broken, the Server checks permissions on each object whose next lower "link" in the chain is owned by a different user. This check of the ownership chain allows the owner of the original data to control access to it.

While this check of the ownership chain promotes data protection by the original owner, it may thwart your attempts to provide that same protection through views and procedures. Be careful and thorough during your design phase to avoid such complications and confusion.

## ⑤ *Using Views as a Security Mechanism*

You can use a view to maintain the normalization of your schema while providing a layer of protection over certain columns of a table. In the previous accounting example (in "Access control via changes to your schema"), you can create a view with only non-sensitive data columns in it and allow all users all accesses to that view. Then you can create another view which contains the sensitive data elements (along with the key) and provide access only to the management staff who need that data.

With the two views created, you can then delegate CRUD accesses in a chart, just as you would for any other database object. Review your new set of access needs and determine whether the views you have created effectively support the least-privilege notion. Be sure you have protected the appropriate columns without hindering needed accesses.

The view mechanism also lets you control access to certain rows or columns within a table. To do this, use a qualifying *where* clause in the view-creation statement. In addition, in SQL Server 10.x, you can create a view with the *with check option* syntax which imposes a view integrity over the data. All data modification statements are validated against the view selection criteria; all rows inserted or updated through the view must remain visible through the view.

While views can provide you with a certain level of data integrity, they may not be the right solution for your protection needs. Certainly, they are one more database object to maintain. And if their underlying object is altered, you must decide whether to change your view definition. Views share a drawback—ownership chains—with stored procedures, which was discussed in the previous section.

# ⑥ *Using Sybase Secure SQL Server*

If, in reviewing your data-integrity needs, you discover that much of your data is sensitive at the row level, and that there are varying levels of sensitivity, consider recommending the Sybase Secure SQL Server. This server, which has all the features of the SQL Server 10.x, provides an additional level of access control known as Mandatory Access Control: access to data rows is strictly determined based on row sensitivity, user clearances, and a system-security policy. If your system has such sensitivity limitations, and they were not properly addressed during the logical design phase, resolve this now.

# ⑦ *Using Multiple Databases*

Review your schema to determine whether you should use multiple databases to gain protections at the database level. An identical database can hold "cover story" information, accessible to users who are not permitted access to the true data.

# ⑧ *Using SQL Server 10.x Security Features*

In SYBASE SQL Server 10.x, you can configure an audit trail to track threats to data integrity such as:
- server logins and logouts
- uses of any commands requiring special authorizations
- uses of commands that refer to a specific object or database
- deletion of objects
- execution of stored procedures and triggers

**125**

- any actions performed by a specified user

This new Server feature, combined with a variety of new identification mechanisms, lets you track data accesses. During the physical-design phase, you may want to confer with the SSO to devise an auditing plan to effectively augment your intended access controls. Be judicious in your use of the audit trail. It may add a needless performance and space burden if you over-audit your users and their activities.

You should also review user-identification mechanisms provided in SQL Server 10.x to plan for their use in your system. Mechanisms to consider are:

- login account locking, to lock a user's account without dropping the user and user's objects from all databases
- systemwide password-expiration option
- client-side password-encryption option
- mechanisms to recover lost or expired passwords

# Epilogue

*The following list summarizes the tasks performed as you determined security and access control mechanisms.*

❶ Considered access and security issues.

❷ Decided who would have system-administration and database-owner privileges. In SQL Server 10.x, decided who would have SA, SSO, and OPER privileges.

❸ Decided which groups of users and individual users will have:
- select privileges
- data-modification privileges
- privileges to execute stored procedures
- privileges to execute commands

❹ Considered using stored procedures to restrict access to data.

❺ Considered using views to restrict access to data.

❻ Considered using Sybase Secure SQL Server.

❼ Considered using multiple databases.

❽ Considered using SQL Server 10.x security features.

# Some things to remember:

▶ A good solution for SA and OPER and SSO responsibilities is to give the SA role to the primary system administrator and then give the same role to one other person, as a backup to the primary. Then designate one primary OPER, and one backup; and designate one primary SSO and one backup.

▶ In a large installation, you may want to appoint a staff of OPER users to support the demands of volume changes for backup and load procedures.

▶ If you decide to lock the *sa* account, be sure to check all scripts that may contain its login and password. Scripts cannot run if they are meant to run as *sa* and that account is locked.

▶ Provide ALL users with their own login names. Do not promote or allow sharing of logins.

▶ When you grant a user access to a database, add that user's name to the database's access list.

▶ Avoid using the *guest* user account. It does not let you know who has access to your data.

▶ Do not give users the *master* database as their default database.

▶ Pay attention to ownership chain issues when using either views or stored procedures as security mechanisms. The SQL Server does not check permissions on any of the underlying objects if the same user owns all of these objects, and if all of the objects are in the same database. Otherwise, they are checked and may constrain access in an unexpected manner.

▶ You may want to confer with the SSO during the physical design phase to devise an effective auditing plan to support your intended access control.

# Chapter 20
## *Managing Object Sizes*

## Prologue

*In this chapter, you will calculate the probable size of a database and its objects.*

**Must you do this activity? Why or when?**

Yes, to make best use of disk space and arrange best placement of objects.

**What do you need before you start? How or where do you get it?**
- Complete table and column definition.
- Complete index definition.
- Estimated number of rows in each table.
- Average length of variable-length fields.

**What are the tasks in this activity?**
① Estimate the size of each table, including the clustered index.
② Estimate the size of each nonclustered index.
③ Consider using average sizes for variable-length columns.
④ Estimate the size of text and image data pages.
⑤ Estimate the size of the transaction log.
⑥ Consider other size factors.

### *Some things to keep in mind*

■ You can drop noncritical indexes if space is an issue.

■ You can remove any redundant, derived, or duplicated data if space is an issue.

# Tasks

*Read through all the tasks in this section before you begin the first task. Perform tasks sequentially, as presented.*

## ① *Estimating the Size of Tables and Clustered Indexes*

Estimating the size of database tables is an important part of physical design. Since your hardware provides a finite space, you need an accurate estimate of the size of your database.

**Note**

To calculate the probable size of a SQL Server table, you need to know the maximum size or expected size of each column. The calculations in this chapter help you plan for the maximum size (worst case) and expected average lengths of the fields.

For pre-SQL Server 10.x releases, Sybase provides algorithms in the *System Administration Guide* for estimating table size. To use them, you need:

- the percentage of rows in which each optional column is present
- the average size of variable-length columns
- the number of rows in each table

SQL Server 10.x provides the system procedure *sp_estspace* which estimates the amount of space required for a table and its indexes, and the time needed to create the index. Consult the *SQL Server Reference Manual: Volume II System Procedures and Catalog Stored Procedures* for further information about the procedure. Additionally, refer to the Datatypes section of the *SQL Server Reference Manual: Volume I Commands, Functions, and Topics* for further detail.

The following steps help you estimate the size of tables and indexes in a database for the SQL Server 4.x family of servers and are currently applicable to SQL Server 10.x servers. Tables containing variable-length columns require more overhead, so two sets of formulas are presented.

The basic process calculates the number of bytes of data, plus overhead, and divides that into the number of bytes available on a data page. Due to page overhead and logging overhead, 2016 bytes are available for row data and row accounting information on a 2K byte data page.

**Note**
The largest single row which may reside on a data page is 1962 bytes.

For best accuracy, *round down* divisions that calculate the number of rows per page and *round up* divisions that calculate the number of pages.

If you are using *fillfactor* in your *create index* statement, it will change some of the equations. See the section on *fillfactor* later in this section.

If your table includes *text* or *image* datatypes, use 16 (the size of the text pointer that is stored in the row) in the following calculations, and then see "Text and Image Data Pages" at the end of this section for additional sizing considerations.

The storage sizes in bytes for SQL Server datatypes are given in Table 20.1.

For sizing purposes, any columns defined as null must be considered variable-length columns, since they involve the same overhead associated with variable-length columns. *numeric* and *decimal* datatypes have a maximum size of 17 bytes.

All of the calculations in the steps that follow are based on the maximum size for *varchar*, *nvarchar*, and *varbinary* data—the defined size for the columns. They also assume that columns were defined as not null.

 **Note**
If you wish to use average values instead, see the section on "Using Average Sizes for Variable Fields."

## Formula 1: Calculating the data-row size

Calculation of data-row size varies depending on whether the row stores any variable-length columns. Use the first formula if all of the columns are fixed length, and defined as not null. Use the second formula if the row contains variable-length columns, or columns defined as null.

**Only Fixed-Length Columns**

    4    (Overhead)

+ _____    Sum of bytes in all fixed-length columns

          = Data-Row Size

**Some Variable-Length Columns**

| | | |
|---|---|---|
| | 4 | (Overhead) |
| + | | Sum of bytes in all fixed-length columns |
| + | | Sum of bytes in all variable-length columns |
| | | = Subtotal |
| + | | (Subtotal / 256) + 1 (overhead) |
| + | | Number of variable-length columns + 1 |
| + | 2 | (Overhead) |
| | | = Data Row Size |

## Table 20.1 SQL Server Datatype Storage Sizes ------------------------------------------

| Datatype | Size in Bytes |
|---|---|
| *char* | Defined size |
| *varchar* | Data size |
| *binary* | Defined size |
| *varbinary* | Data size |
| *int* | 4 |
| *smallint* | 2 |
| *tinyint* | 1 |
| *numeric* | 2 + (precision/2) |
| *decimal* | 2 + (precision/2) |
| *double precision* | 8 |
| *float* | 8 |
| *real* | 4 |
| *money* | 8 |
| *smallmoney* | 4 |
| *datetime* | 8 |
| *smalldatetime* | 4 |

Table 20.1 (continued) ----------------------------------------------------------------------------

| Datatype | Size in Bytes |
|----------|---------------|
| *bit* | 1 |
| *text* | minimum 16 + 2K per initialized column |
| *image* | minimum 16 + 2K per initialized column |
| *timestamp* | 8 |
| *nchar* | Defined size * @@*ncharsize* |
| *nvarchar* | Data size * @@*nvarcharsize* |

*Table 1.1 of this book provides more detail about datatypes.*

## Formula 2: Calculating the number of data pages

This is a two-part calculation:

2016/Data Row Size = Number of Data Rows Per Page

Number of Rows/Rows Per Page = Number of Data Pages Required

## Formula 3: Calculating the size of clustered-index rows

Calculation of the size of clustered-index rows depends on whether the keys are fixed or variable length. Use the first formula if all the keys are fixed length. Use the second formula if keys include variable-length columns.

**Fixed-Length Only**

|       | |
|-------|---|
| 5 | Overhead |
| + _____ | Sum of bytes in the fixed-length index keys |
|       | = Clustered Row Size |

**Some Variable-Length Columns**

|       | |
|-------|---|
| 5 | Overhead |
|       | Sum of bytes in the fixed-length index keys |
| + _____ | Sum of bytes in the variable-length index keys |

**133**

**Some Variable-Length Columns (continued)**

|   |   |   |
|---|---|---|
|   | Subtotal |   |
| + _____ | (Subtotal / 256) + 1 |   |
| + ____2 | Overhead |   |
|   | = Clustered-Index Row Size |   |

## Formula 4: Calculating the number of clustered-index pages

This is a two-part calculation, where the second calculation is a loop:

(2016 / Clustered Row Size) - 2 = Number of Clustered-Index (CI) Rows Per Page

Number of Data Pages/ Number of CI Rows per Page= Number of Index Pages at Level 0

If the result above is > 1, repeat the following division step, using the quotient as the next dividend, until the quotient = 1, which means that you have reached the root level of the index:

Number of Index Pages / Number of CI Rows per Page = Number of Index Pages

at Last Levelat Next Level

## Formula 5: Calculating the total number of pages

Totals:

|   |   |
|---|---|
| Index Level(s) | Pages: |
| 2 |   |
| 1 |   |
| 0 |   |
| Data (Level 0) | + _____ |
|   | = Total Number of Data Pages |

## Formula 6: Calculating allocation overhead and total pages

Each table, and each index on a table, has an Object Allocation Map (OAM). The OAM is stored on pages allocated to the table or index. A single page of an OAM holds allocation mapping for between 2016 and 64,260 pages of data or index.

Number of Data Pages / 64,260 = Minimum OAM Pages

Number of Data Pages / 2,016 = Maximum OAM Pages

Number of Index Pages / 64,260 = Minimum OAM Pages

Number of Index Pages / 2,016 = Maximum OAM Pages

|  | Minimum | Maximum |
|---|---|---|
| Clustered-Index Pages | _____ | _____ |
| Index OAM Pages | _____ | _____ |
| Data Pages | _____ | _____ |
| Data OAM Pages | +_____ | +_____ |
| Total Pages Needed | _____ | _____ |

## ② *Estimating the Size of Nonclustered Indexes*

Size tables and clustered indexes first; then size the nonclustered indexes. This is a six-step process.

## Formula 7: Calculating the size of the leaf-index row

Calculation of the size of nonclustered index rows depends on whether the keys are fixed or variable length. Use the first formula if all the keys are fixed length. Use the second formula if keys include variable-length columns.

**Fixed-length Keys Only**

|  |  |
|---|---|
| 7 | Overhead |
| +_____ | Sum of Fixed-Length Keys |
|  | =Size of Leaf Index Row |

**Some Variable-length Keys**

| | |
|---|---|
| 9 | Overhead |
| + | Sum of length of fixed-length keys |
| ± | Sum of length of variable-length keys |
| + | Number of variable-length keys +1 |
| | =Subtotal |
| + | (Subtotal / 256) + 1 |
| | =Size of Leaf Index Row |

## Formula 8: Calculating the number of leaf pages in the index

This is a two-part calculation:

2016 / Size of Leaf Index Row = Number of Leaf Rows per Page

Number of Rows in Table / Number of Leaf Rows per Page = Number of Leaf Pages

## Formula 9: Calculating the size of the nonleaf rows

| | | |
|---|---|---|
| | | Size of Leaf Index Row |
| + | 4 | Overhead |
| | | = Size of Nonleaf Row |

## Formula 10: Calculating the number of nonleaf pages

This is a two-part calculation, where the second part is a loop:

(2016 / Size of Nonleaf Row) - 2 = Number of Nonleaf Index Rows per Page

Number of Leaf Pages / Number of Nonleaf Index Rows Per Page = Number of Index Pages at Level 1

If the result above is > 1, repeat the following division step, using the quotient as the next dividend, until the quotient = 1, which means that you have reached the root level of the index:

| Number of Index Pages | / | Number of Nonleaf at Last Level | = | Number of Index Pages Index Rows Per Pageat Next Level |
|---|---|---|---|---|

## Formula 11: Computing the number of nonleaf index pages

Totals:

| Index Level(s) | Pages |
|---|---|
| 4 | |
| 3 | |
| 2 | |
| 1 | |
| 0 | + _____ |

= Total Number of 2K Data Pages Used

## Formula 12: Calculating allocation overhead and total pages

Number of Index Pages / 64,260 = Minimum OAM Pages

Number of Index Pages / 2016 = Maximum OAM Pages

| | Minimum | Maximum |
|---|---|---|
| Nonclustered Index Pages | | |
| OAM Pages | +_____ | +_____ |
| Total Pages Needed: | | |

# ③ *Considering Using Average Sizes for Variable-Length Columns*

The calculations outlined in Step 1 and Step 2 use the maximum size of the variable-length columns. If you know the average size of the columns, you can use this value in calculating table size and index sizes as follows:

**In Formula 1:**

Use the sum of the average length of the variable-length columns instead of the sum of the defined (maximum) length of the variable-length columns to determine the Average Data Row Size.

**In Formula 2:**

Use the Average Data Row Size from Formula 1 in the first part of the calculation.

**In Formula 3:**

You must perform the addition twice. The first time, calculate the *Maximum Index Row Size*, using the given formula. The second time calculate the *Average Index Row Size*, substituting the sum of the average number of bytes in the variable-length index keys for the sum of the defined (maximum) number of bytes in the variable-length index keys.

**In Formula 4:**

Substitute this formula for the first part in Step 1D, using the two different size values from Step 1C:

(2016-2 * *Maximum_Size*) / *Average_Size* = Number of Clustered IndexRows Per Page

**In Formula 7:**

You must perform the addition twice. The first time, calculate the *Maximum Leaf Index Row Size*, using the given formula. The second time, calculate the *Average Leaf Index Row Size*, substituting the average number of bytes in the variable-length index keys for the sum of bytes in the variable-length index keys.

**In Formula 8:**

Substitute this formula for the first part in Step 2B, using the two different size values from Step 2A:

(2016-2 * *Maximum_Size*) / *Average_Size* = Number of Leaf Rows Per Page

**In Formula 9:**

You must perform the addition twice. The first time, calculate the *Maximum Nonleaf Index Row Size*, using the given formula. The second time, calculate the *Average Nonleaf Index Row Size*, substituting the average number of bytes in the variable-length index keys for the sum of bytes in the variable-length index keys.

**In Formula 10:**

Substitute this formula for the first part in Step 2D, using the two different size values calculated in Step 2C:

(2016-2**Maximum_Size*)/*Average_Size* = Number of Nonleaf Index Rows Per Page

## ④ *Estimating the Size of* Text *and* Image *Data Pages*

Each *text* or *image* column stores a 16-byte pointer in the data row, with the datatype *varchar(16)*. Each text or image column that is initialized requires at least 2K bytes (one data page) of storage space.

*Text* and *image* columns are designed to store "implicit" null values, meaning that the text pointer in the data row remains null, and no text page is initialized for the value, saving 2K of storage space.

If you define a *text* or *image* column to allow null values, and create the row with an *insert* statement that includes null for the *text* or *image* column, SQL Server initializes no column, and you save space.

If a *text* or *image* column is changed in any way with an *update*, then the text page is allocated. Of course, *insert*s or *update*s that place actual data in a column initialize the page.

The text chains that store *text* and *image* data have 112 bytes of overhead per page. To calculate the number of *text* chain pages that a particular entry will use, apply this formula:

Data Length / 1800 = Number of 2K Pages

Round the result *up* in all cases; that is, a data length of 1801 bytes requires two 2K pages.

## ⑤ *Estimating the Size of the Transaction Log*

The size of the device required for the transaction log (the *syslogs* table) varies according to the amount of logged activity (*insert*s, *update*s, *delete*s) and the frequency of transaction log dumps. Update activity increases the size of the logs, and *dump transaction* decreases the size of the log by writing committed transactions to disk and removing them from the log.

As a rule of thumb, allocate 10% to 25% of the space you allocate to the database itself to the log. In a database that is frequently modified, the log can grow quite large, so once your database is in use, monitor the size of your log until you can see how much space it needs.

## ⑥ *Considering Other Factors in Estimating Sizes*

Besides the concerns about total database size, consider these other factors which affect your table creations.

## When *fillfactor* = 100

The index management process normally leaves room for two additional rows on each index page. When you set *fillfactor* to 100%, it no longer leaves room for these rows. This affects your calculations for the number of clustered index pages and for the number of nonleaf pages. In both cases, you normally subtract two from the number of rows per page; with *fillfactor* at 100%, skip that calculation.

## Other *fillfactor* values

Other values for *fillfactor* reduce the number of rows per page on data pages and leaf index pages. To compute the correct values when using *fillfactor*, multiply the size of the available data page (2016) by the *fillfactor*. For example, if your *fillfactor* is 75%, your data page would hold 1512 bytes. Use this value in place of 2016.

## Distribution pages

SQL Server creates a distribution page when you create an index on existing data, and when you run *update statistics*. A distribution page occupies one full data page.

The *update statistics* command adds one distribution page for each index on which statistics have been created. If you update statistics for an entire table, allow one page in your estimate for each index on the table. If you update statistics for only one index, add one.

## Very small rows

SQL Server can't store more than 256 data or index rows on a page. Even if your rows are extremely short, the minimum number of data pages will be:

Number of Rows / 256 = Number of Data Pages Required

# Epilogue

*The following list summarizes the tasks performed as you managed object sizes.*

❶ Estimated the size of each table, including the clustered index.
❷ Estimated the size of each nonclustered index.

❸ Considered using average sizes for variable-length columns.
❹ Estimated the size of text and image data pages.
❺ Estimated the size of the transaction log.
❻ Considered other size factors.

# *Some things to remember:*

▶ The largest single row which may reside on a data page is 1962 bytes.

▶ Each data page and index page has 2016 bytes available for data or index rows.

▶ Each *text* or *image* column stores a 16-byte pointer in the data row, with the datatype *varchar(16)*. Each text or image column that is initialized requires at least 2K bytes (one data page) of storage space.

# Chapter 21

# *Recommending Object Placement*

## Prologue

*In this chapter, you will allocate databases and their objects on available hardware to achieve best performance.*

**Must you do this activity? Why or when?**

Yes, if estimated performance requirements may not be met.

**What do you need before you start? How or where do you get it?**

- Complete table and column definition.
- Complete index definition.
- Database and object sizes.
- Target hardware.
- Recovery requirements.
- Knowledge and understanding of application transactions.

**What are the tasks in this activity?**

① Identify critical database transactions which may compete with each other for resources. Identify tables, columns, and indexes accessed in those transactions.

② Consider using SQL Server devices to improve performance and recovery.

③ Consider using multiple databases.

④ Consider using SQL Server segments to improve performance.

⑤ Consider using SQL Server mirroring to improve performance and recovery.

## Some things to keep in mind

■ Performance testing and system administration may require you to reallocate databases and their objects.

# Tasks

*Read through all the tasks in this section before you begin the first task. Perform tasks sequentially, as presented.*

### ① *Identifying Critical Database Transactions*

Physical allocation is the placement of databases and their objects on available hardware. SQL Server makes reasonable default decisions about many aspects of storage management—including where to place databases, tables, and indexes, and how much space is allocated for each of them. However, you can enhance system performance and ensure database recovery by making certain changes in SQL Server's allocation of space to databases and its placement of database objects.

Your physical allocation should:

- improve system performance by distributing disk traffic across all available resources
- guarantee complete recovery after disk crashes.

You must analyze the critical database transactions to see:

- their distribution with respect to time
- which tables and indexes they use
- how many rows are being inserted, updated, and deleted.

You can improve your physical allocation using devices, databases, segments, and mirroring.

### ② *Using Devices*

A database device is any piece of disk or file in the file system that you use to store databases and database objects. The term "device" does not necessarily refer to a distinct physical piece of hardware.

**Note**

Devices in UNIX may be disk files or raw partitions. It's always a good idea to use raw disk partitions. With raw partitions, a write operation is always flushed directly to the disk. With a UNIX file, writes to disk are buffered and may not be written to disk immediately. If SQL Server completes a transaction and sends the result to a UNIX file, the transaction is considered complete even though the UNIX buffer cache may not have been written to disk. If the system crashes before this buffer cache is written, you lose data. In this situation, SQL Server has no way of knowing that the write to disk eventually failed, therefore it does not roll back the transaction.

You can improve system performance by placing logs and database objects on separate devices which are on separate physical disks:

- Place the transaction log on its own device.

    The transaction log is written for every modification; therefore, placing the transaction log on its own device reduces the disk-head movement.

**Note**

This configuration also lets the database administrator dump the transaction log separately from the database. This helps ensure up-to-date recovery after a media failure.

- Place nonclustered indexes and their tables on different devices which are on separate physical disks.

    By placing a table on one disk, and its nonclustered indexes on another, you speed up physical reads and writes, since the work is split between two disk drives.

- Split large tables across devices.

    Splitting large tables across disks improves performance, by reducing contention for disks. This is especially useful in multi-user applications.

- Place a database or object on a different device from its mirror, ensuring that the device is on a different disk and the disk is on a separate disk controller.

    Placing a database or object on one physical disk and its mirror on another reduces read time, since both devices are active.

## ③ *Using Multiple Databases*

You can use a second database to separate:

- active data from archival data
- online transaction-processing application from a decision support application.

**WARNING!**

Putting user databases on the *master* device could result in their erasure. SQL Server may overwrite user databases whenever you run **buildmaster**.

# ④ *Using Segments*

A segment is a named subset of the database devices available to a particular SQL Server database. Think of a segment as a label that points to one or more database devices. Using segments can increase SQL Server performance, and can provide increased control over placement and space usage of specific database objects.

You can improve system performance by placing database objects on separate segments:

- Place nonclustered indexes and their tables on different segments.

  If you place a table on one segment on a device, and its nonclustered indexes on a segment on another disk controller, you may cut down read/write time, since disk- head travel is usually reduced.

- Split large tables across segments.

  If you split a large, heavily used table across segments across two disk controllers, you may shorten read/write time.

- Separate *text* and *image* columns from tables.

  The data for *text* and *image* columns is stored on a separate chain of data pages. By default, this text chain is placed on the same segment as the table. Since reading a text column requires a read operation for the text pointer in the database and an additional read operation for the text page in the separate text chain, you can improve performance by placing the text chain on a separate physical device.

- Control space used by user objects.

  If specific users are instructed to place their tables and indexes on specific segments only, those database objects cannot grow beyond the space available to the devices represented by those segments. Moreover, the objects' space is protected from encroachment by other user-created objects. In an environment where many users have create permissions within a database and where certain tables are considered critical to all users, place the critical tables on segments, and let the users have the default space.

**Note**
SQL Server 10.x can monitor the amount of space left on any segment in a database and execute a stored procedure when the amount of space used rises above a particular percentage, called a threshold. Consult the SQL Server 10.x System Administration Guide's "Managing Free Space with Thresholds" chapter for further information.

# ⑤ *Using Device Mirroring*

Device mirroring allows a SQL Server database device to be duplicated: all writes to the device are copied to a separate physical device. If one fails, the other contains an up-to-date copy of all transactions. Device mirroring provides nonstop recovery in the event of media failure.

**WARNING!**
Mirroring a device increases the time needed to write transactions. Applications involving many writes may be slower with disk mirroring than without it.

Consider three options for mirroring:

- Mirror the transaction-log device.

  This is the minimum guaranteed configuration for database recovery in case of hardware failure. If the disk with the user database fails, you can restore the user database on a new disk from your backups and the mirrored transaction log.

- Mirror all devices.

  This is the completely redundant configuration. It provides nonstop recovery from hardware failure and keeps the system up and running. Working copies of the master and user databases and the log are all mirrored, so that a hardware failure does not interrupt SQL Server users.

  However, this approach requires a lot of storage space, which may be costly.

- Mirror selected devices.

  You select critical devices in addition to the transaction-log device for mirroring. This approach provides complete recovery and some degree of nearly continuous availability.

In summary, the three options have different cost and performance trade-offs. Which is best for you depends on the application's tolerance for system downtime and speed of recovery, availability of storage media, and performance requirements.

# Epilogue

*The following list summarizes the tasks performed as you allocated databases and their objects on available hardware to achieve best performance.*

❶ Identified critical database transactions which may compete with each other for resources. Identified tables, columns, and indexes accessed in those transactions.

❷ Considered using SQL Server devices to improve performance and recovery.

❸ Considered using multiple databases.

❹ Considered using SQL Server segments to improve performance.

❺ Considered using SQL Server mirroring to improve performance and recovery.

## *Some things to remember:*

▶ Devices in UNIX may be disk files or raw partitions. It's always a good idea to use raw disk partitions. With raw partitions, a write operation is always flushed directly to the disk. With a UNIX file, writes to disk are buffered and may not be written to disk immediately.

▶ Keeping the transaction log on a different device than the data lets the database administrator dump the transaction log separately from the database. This helps ensure up-to-date recovery after a media failure.

▶ Putting user databases on the *master* device could result in their erasure. SQL Server may overwrite user databases whenever you run **buildmaster**.

▶ SQL Server 10.x can monitor the amount of space left on any segment in a database and execute a stored procedure when the amount of space remaining shrinks below a particular value, called a threshold. Consult the SQL Server 10.x System Administration Guide's "Managing Free Space with Thresholds" chapter for further information.

▶ Mirroring a device increases the time needed to write transactions. Applications involving many writes may be slower with disk mirroring than without it.

# Appendix A
## *The Sybase Development Framework and MethodSet*

## Executive Summary _____

- Organizations need a new, practical approach in order to ensure quality in the design, development, deployment, and operation of systems based upon the client/server architecture.

- Sybase Worldwide Professional Services has embarked on a two-track program to provide consultants and customers with the methodology to develop client/server systems in a controllable, repeatable, and predictable fashion. The Sybase Development Framework (SDF) is an iterative software development process containing phases, activities, deliverables, and roles.

- Concurrent with the Framework development, a set of detailed, technical methods—the Sybase MethodSet—is being developed and published. These methods address crucial aspects of client/server development by presenting each technical practice as a set of ordered steps along with the underlying rationale. The first of the methods in the MethodSet is *Physical Database Design for SYBASE SQL Server*. Appendix E holds the contents of another technical work in the MethodSet, *Naming Guidelines for SYBASE SQL Server*.

- The methods in the MethodSet are developed for use within the Sybase Development Framework. They may also be appropriate within another development framework or methodology. By uncoupling these components, Sybase can provide an "open methodology."

## What are the advantages of Sybase's approach? _

The methods in the Sybase MethodSet provide a level of detail and depth not generally available in a methodology—even in those designed to support mature technologies. These methods are technical practices developed and refined by Sybase consultants and project managers who have proven these techniques in the field. They provide technical guidance and expertise specific to the Sybase product set. By capturing this expertise in formal methods, we are able to efficiently convey it to our consultants and to our customers.

The Sybase Development Framework is a life cycle definition that is populated with technical methods; it is based on an iterative model. This model is highly conducive to the development of enterprise-wide systems that combine components and technologies in new and unproven ways—including the incorporation of legacy systems. It emphasizes iterative requirements analysis and makes extensive use of prototyping. This approach enables the refinement of requirements to take place as—in each iteration—we discover more about both the problem domain and the capabilities of the tools employed.

An adaptable framework—along with a set of detailed technical methods—is a powerful combination: it is rigorous in its consistency, accountability, and repeatability, yet flexible enough to allow organizations to adopt new technology and techniques.

# What do we mean by "open methodology"?

Sybase understands that many of our customers have large investments in existing methodologies. Sybase's approach enables our customers to preserve and extend their existing investments in methodology, while gaining the benefits of client/server specific techniques.

The methods in the Sybase MethodSet are produced with the expectation that technical practices to support client/server may need to coexist with technical practices developed for other technologies. Further, both sets of technical practices may need to map to a single, standard development methodology. The individual methods in the Sybase MethodSet are constructed to easily map to numerous existing methodologies, as well as to the Sybase Development Framework.

Similarly, if our customers use the Sybase Development Framework as the driving methodology, both Sybase and non-Sybase methods and techniques may be employed using the same overall life cycle definition.

# History

Single-server, homogeneous client/server systems of the late 1980s were developed and managed very much like their predecessors, the host-based systems. Developers and system integrators at that time still envisioned the development process as a series of one-time activities, roughly consisting of: requirements definition, preliminary design, detailed design, development, test, and deployment.

Figure A.1 The waterfall approach --------------------------------------------------------

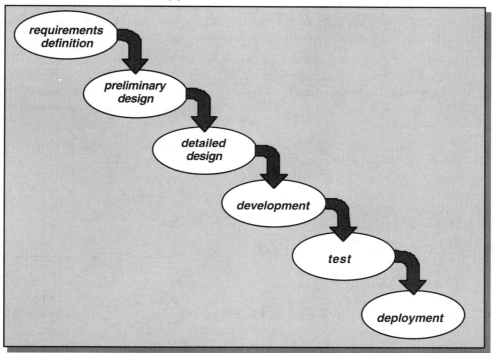

Though variants of "the waterfall approach," pictured in Figure A.1, currently exist, they provide limited means by which to conduct the early prototyping or proof-of-concept trials needed to evaluate the numerous possible configurations within the client/server paradigm, and to build up—through iterations—a stable and appropriate system.

These more complex architectures need more opportunities for trial, more opportunities for definition and redefinition, and more opportunities to design and redesign *before* final development and deployment.

Both customers and consultants have been seeking a structure to capture and maintain an iterative approach that will reduce the risk associated with enterprise-wide client/server systems. While informal methods have begun to emerge from the existing expertise, such a collection of practices does not guarantee successful implementation.

Additionally, the waterfall and its variations do not address or manage the true complexity that client/server architectures can entail. These approaches do not recognize and maintain all the various components—both hardware and software—that can make up a system. As a result, such methodologies cannot aid developers in allocating their requirements to various components and then in successfully integrating the pieces into a cohesive system.

In reviewing existing process models for software development, we are drawn to those that possess two characteristics: those that are iterative—especially in the areas of requirements discovery and design—and those that make effective use of prototyping. None, however, seems specifically suited for development of client/server systems.

Sybase has therefore determined to develop its own software development process model for the successful development of both department-level and enterprise-wide client/server systems.

# The Rationale Behind the Sybase Development Framework

Experience has demonstrated that a development process for client/server should be based upon iterations of a cycle containing identification of requirements, design and definition of functional components, construction and integration of these components, and evaluation of the resulting system.

We believe this is true for two particular reasons: first, there is an unprecedented number of choices in tools and technology. Evaluating combinations early—when the cost of making changes is less—can mitigate project risk. Second, complex problems often cannot be sufficiently defined without beginning the solution process. Incremental or iterative approaches allow design and prototyping activities to contribute to the discovery of full and meaningful specifications.

As illustrated in Figure A.2, the process is a cycle of four phases:

- *Identify* needs and opportunities
- *Design* and allocate functional components
- *Construct* and integrate components
- *Evaluate* the results

Figure A.2 A cyclic development process ---------------------------------------------

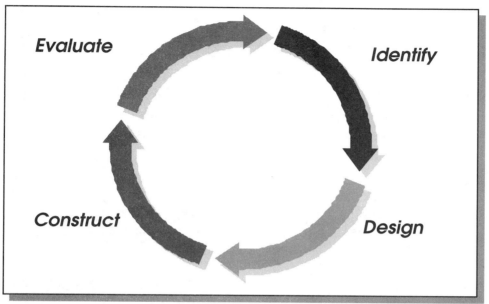

This process differs from previous development models. We no longer simply gather requirements, design a series of flowcharts, write code, test, and deploy. Development for client/server also includes choosing platforms, tools, and locations for functions and data. These choices are best made with the information provided by trials; the development model must reflect this need.

## The need for progress

While this cycle works well to support the discovery and trial needed in client/server development, it can be endless. Organizations need to show *progress*. That is, each successive cycle through the process brings a greater level of refinement, optimization, and constraint, based upon the results of the previous cycle(s) of the process. This is referred to as cycle progression.

Progress may be expressed and tracked as:

- refinement
- accumulation
- constraint
- level of detail
- fitness

This is illustrated in Figure A.3.

**Figure A.3 The progress model** ----------------------------------------------------------------

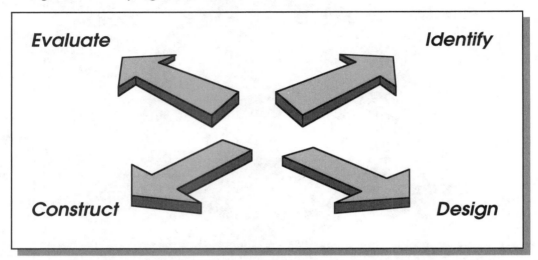

For example, requirements identification will progress from general objectives and high-level business terms to very detailed module requirements. Designs and models will become increasingly detailed, constrained, and optimized through successive iterations. Prototypes will change by covering more of the requisite functionality or by handling identified risks with more rigor. Repositories will accumulate entries—entities in data dictionaries, objects, or code templates in libraries. Evaluation criteria and test plans will change and adapt along with the system.

## The need for control

Iterative—but unbridled—cycles may show progress. But, for production-software development projects, the iteration through the cycles must be a *controlled* progression, as shown in Figure A.4. Organizations need a predictable process upon which to base budgets, schedules, staffing, and plans.

This requisite control can be exercised by defining:

- phases
- activities and tasks
- deliverables

Figure A.4 Controlled progression ----------------------------------------------------------

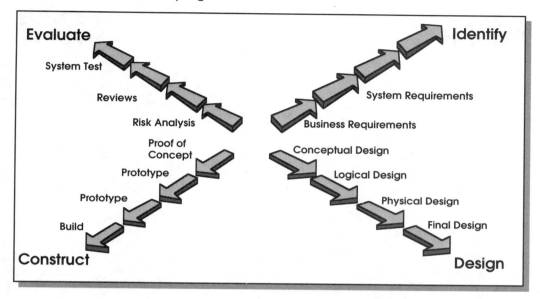

- dependencies
- roles

In order to control the software development process, each activity must be rigorously defined. The control and built-in progression of the client/server development process are, therefore, expressed as well-defined tasks and deliverables.

The relationship between activities in successive cycles must also be well-defined. For example, the design of client/server systems demands a well-defined transition from logical to physical models in order to ensure the most appropriate allocation of functions across the network.

## The Sybase Development Framework

The combination of repeated cycles and outward, controlled progression can be modeled as a spiral, as shown in Figure A.5. The process begins at the center-point. As the project proceeds and the spiral forms, the system's growth and refinement are represented by increases in the diameter of the spiral.

Figure A.5 The Sybase Development Framework spiral

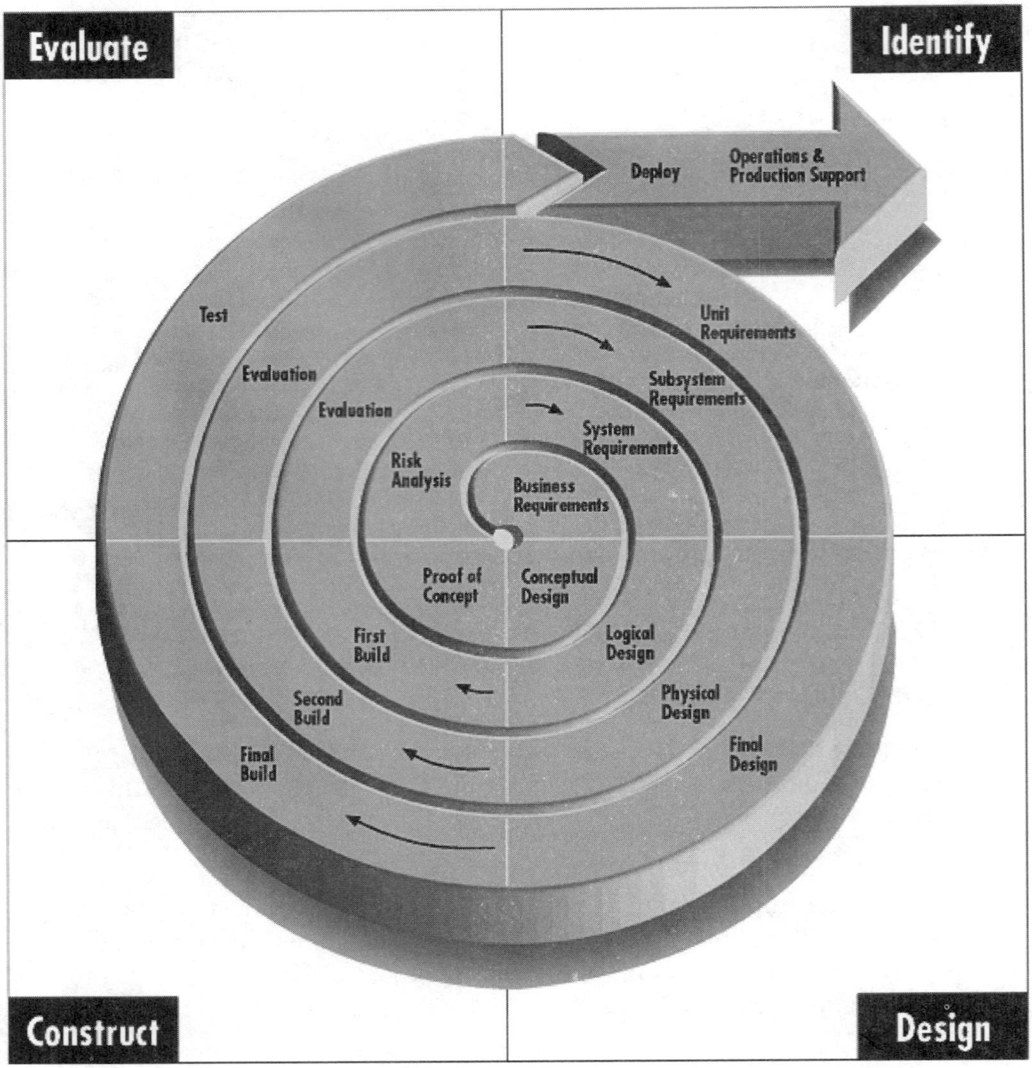

As Figure A.5 conveys, the Sybase Development Framework combines a cyclic development process, the progression of iterations, and the control of cycles into defined activities, which in turn produce deliverables. The final and crucial deliverable is the system.

This framework definition allows for both abbreviation and extension as determined appropriate by project managers for each application of the approach. This makes the Sybase Development Framework appropriate for both large and small projects. It also allows the variable management of risk by the amount and depth of prototyping that are loaded into the early cycles.

The scopes of the prototypes are determined during the identification phase of each cycle. They may range from superficial mockups of screens and reports to production quality subsets of the entire application. The prototypes may be used to incrementally construct the entire system, or to target discrete areas of functional or technical risk.

Also, each cycle includes an evaluation process that determines if the system is ready to proceed to the next cycle. During this review process, the project team re-evaluates the goals and requirements of the system in light of the information discovered during the preceding design and prototyping activities from this cycle.

Therefore, to be assured of success, projects need to follow an appropriate process model *and* be guided through the activities by detailed technical methods.

The Sybase Development Framework forms a well-defined software development process that meets management's need for control. The Sybase MethodSet provides technical guidance to designers and developers of client/server systems.

An adaptable framework—along with a set of detailed technical methods—is a powerful combination; it is rigorous in its consistency, accountability, and repeatability, yet flexible enough to allow organizations to adopt new technology and techniques.

# Appendix B
## *A Sample Database*

*The sample database* pubs *is used in examples throughout this text. The model in Figure B.1 represents the* pubs *database's logical design after some denormalization has been applied. The column, total_sales, in the titles table, is a derived column.*

Figure B.1 The *pubs* database

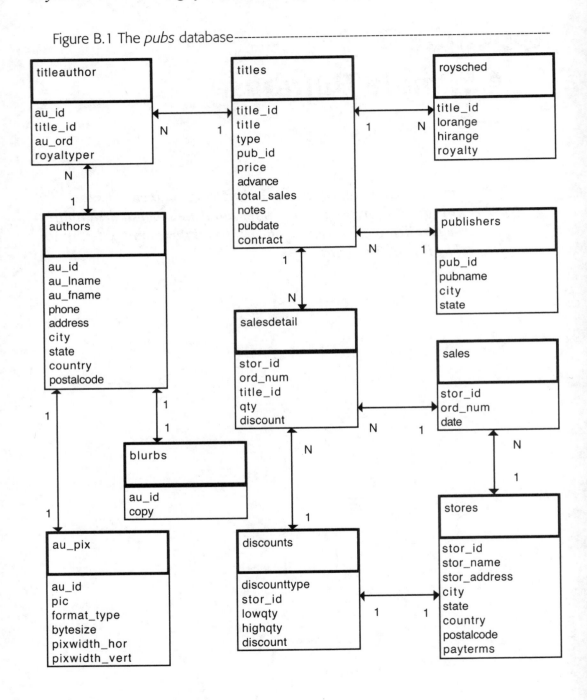

# Appendix C
## *Required Inputs to Physical Database Design*

*The process of physical database design transforms a logical database design or model into an* implementable *and* optimized *database design. The resulting physical database design provides for all application and processing requirements.*

You can use this appendix as a checklist to determine whether you are ready to do physical database design. Additionally, the Sybase Development Framework and Sybase MethodSet, described in Appendix A, provide guidance in performing physical database design within a complete software development effort.

## Preceding Phases and Activities

Phases and activities that precede the physical design phase include:

- Requirements Discovery and Analysis
- Logical Design

You may revisit these phases after completing a physical design.

## Following Phases and Activities

Phases and activities that generally follow the Physical Design phase include:

- Prototyping and Planning
- Unit Development
- Unit Test

- Integration Test
- System Test
- Acceptance Test
- Deployment
- Operations and Production Support

# Documents from the Requirements Analysis ___

You should have the following documents available to you upon completion of the Requirements Analysis activities:

- System functional requirements
- Performance and availability requirements
- Security requirements
- Organizational constraints

## System functional requirements

The System Functional Requirements document lists the function points that the system will support. This document specifies the domain of functions to be implemented. It is typically a subset of functions identified in a Business Requirements document.

The functional requirements should contain a succinct, numbered list of function points that can be tracked and referred to in subsequent documents. This is the basis for requirements tracking, and for the ultimate acceptance of the system.

Each function point tells what the design must do, not how.

For example,

*"The system shall track the time and nature of each deviation from the product specifications"*

is a valid requirement.

*"The system shall add one to the deviation counter and log the temperature and pressure at the time of the deviation to the printer"*

is not a valid requirement, but is part of the design process.

## Performance and availability requirements

The Performance and Availability Requirements document states the response-time and throughput requirements. Maximum, average, and desired

162

response characteristics are specified. System availability and redundancy requirements are also specified. Maximum, average, and desired fail-over times are presented here.

Vague or under-specified performance requirements such as, "The system shall perform with adequate response time for all operations" are not appropriate. A more appropriate requirement would be, "The average response time for queries supported by the user interface shall be less than 3 seconds."

Performance requirements should be realistic in terms of cost to implement. For example, "The system shall be available twenty-four (24) hours a day, seven (7) days a week. Failure of any software or hardware component shall not cause the system to be unavailable for more than one (1) minute" could be a valid requirement. However, the cost of implementing such a system would be substantial.

## Security requirements

The Security Requirements document specifies the levels of security to be implemented and the objects to be secured. Secured resources can include networks, computers, applications, functions, data, and procedures.

Security requirements are often overly complex. Limit your security requirements to the essential.

## Organizational constraints

You may face organizational constraints that limit your design choices. These constraints may include budgetary limitations or time limitations. Document them in order to track their effect on the overall Logical Design and eventual Physical Design.

# Logical Design Documents

The Logical Design Document presents a view of the system to be implemented, with minimal regard to the physical constraints of the target environment. It will delineate the conceptual relationship and the communication amongst the software and data components of the system.

The Logical Database Design should be highly normalized, at least to third-normal form. This is the document that will provide a direct linkage between the enterprise logical data model (usually an entity relationship diagram) and the business model (usually a data flow diagram or process model). It should refer to those documents if they exist.

# Logical entity relationship diagram (ERD)

The Logical Entity Relationship Diagram will contain a graphic representation of the entities that will be instantiated as tables in the physical database design. This diagram should contain, at a minimum, the entity names and the cardinality between them. Include attributes, keys, and common join criteria.

To create this diagram, use a CASE tool. At a minimum, a computer drawing tool should be used.

# Entities

Each entity should have a textual description of the object that it is intended to model.

For entity names, use complete words separated by underscores— "factory_configuration" rather than "fact_conf." Use abbreviations only when they are commonly used, for example, "nbr" for number. Do not attempt to keep table names arbitrarily short to save keystrokes. Extra keystrokes are worthwhile in a data model that can be intuitively understood at first glance. (You can always use an alias at development time to reduce keystrokes.)

# Attributes

The attribute list will contain each attribute in each entity including its data type, domain, and whether a null value is allowed.

Use complete, meaningful words as attribute names (as with entity names).

# Domains

Specify the set of valid domains for the system here. Domains can be expressed as ranges, lists, regular expressions (picture strings), or as combinations of these.

# Referential integrity

The referential integrity section of the logical database design will contain the general approach to referential integrity. It will specify the allowability of primary-key updates, cascading key updates, and cascading deletes. In addition, it will specify the relationships between the entities' keys in the logical design, and the constraints on *inserts*, *updates*, and *deletes* based on other table populations.

164

## Primary and foreign keys

Each entity will have a primary key that will uniquely identify each row. Foreign keys that participate in each entity will also be specified.

## Security

The Logical Database Security Design will specify the levels of security for each user with respect to column and table read, write, and delete. Any entities that support additional security requirements (such as user profiles or value-oriented security) will be described here.

## Size estimates

For each entity, estimate the number of rows. If the number of rows will vary over time, the time frames and factors affecting the row populations should be specified.

This task will help you with the overall sizing of system components such as disk drives, disk controllers, and memory and network bandwidth requirements.

## Prototypes

The purpose of the proof-of-concept prototype is to demonstrate the feasibility of an architectural approach or a set of tools or configurations to meet the requirements. Use prototyping when you are trying to use new tools or technologies, or when technology or business requirements have shifted so much that you need new application architectures and approaches.

The goal of the proof of concept prototype is to establish feasibility and to discover the strengths and weaknesses of the proposed tools and configurations. This knowledge is critical to the later design phases. Prototyping should not be an attempt to complete a portion of the system early. While portions of software developed in this phase may be useful during implementation, this is not its primary purpose. Unit development must be based on physical design.

# Transaction Characterization

Any changes to data within a database are made by means of transactions. You must analyze the transactions occurring within an application. This analysis will help you to design the database so that it supports the high-value transactions of the application.

You can make a logical process model to graphically depict the transactions occurring in an application. This document contains a logical representation of the functions to be performed by various subsystems. The document shows the business events and the transactions that flow between the subsystems. Some customers have used Data Flow Diagrams to depict transaction flow in an application.

In analyzing transactions, remember the 80/20 rule. Twenty percent of the transactions are usually responsible for 80% of the system throughput. These transactions are the high-value transactions of the application.

Transaction analysis should thus include:

- most frequent transactions
- transactions affecting many rows
- transactions affecting many tables
- resource-intensive transactions

Design your physical database to support these transactions.

You must also analyze the distribution of transactions with respect to time. This information is especially useful if the distribution is not uniform. For example, an application may have seasonal or periodic processing, or peak periods at certain times of the day.

In an online transaction processing application, ad hoc access to data may be infrequent. However, ad hoc analysis is important in a decision-support system and you should find out what type of ad hoc analysis may occur.

# Logical Database Design Acceptance

Your Logical Database Design should be reviewed by a committee of analysts and designers to ensure that:

- the system's requirements are being met
- the design represents a logical view of the data
- all requisite information for the physical design is present in the logical design or in the requirements documents.

Any deficiencies, errors, or inconsistencies in database design or any design elements which are outside the scope of the required system should be reported to the authors of the Logical Database Design document.

Once the Logical Database Design document has been corrected, the committee should review it again.

# Appendix D
## *Physical Database Design Deliverables*

*Deliverables from the physical database design process should include a graphic representation of the database in the form of an Entity Relationship Diagram (ERD) and textual descriptions of the database design in the form of a Physical Database Design Document.*

## Physical Entity Relationship Diagram (ERD) _____

The Physical Entity Relationship Diagram (ERD) contains a graphic representation of the tables in the physical database design. The Physical ERD should be a physical representation of the Logical ERD. This ERD must contain, at a minimum, the table names and the relationships between tables including cardinality and optionality. It should also include columns, keys, and common join criteria. This ERD should represent any strategic denormalization used to achieve business or performance goals.

For tables and columns that correspond one-to-one with their logical counterparts, use the same names.

You must maintain and distribute the physical ERD throughout the design and development process. You can use the Deft ERD editor to create the physical ERD.

## Physical Database Design Document _____

In the Physical Database Design Document you must include textual descriptions that complement the Physical Database Design ERD. In a large application, the physical ERD should be partitioned into a number of smaller diagrams by subject area, though not all tools support this operation. You can use a tool such as the Deft ERD Report to produce the design document.

## Tables

Each table specification must include a textual description of the object that the table is intended to model. The specification should also include the entity or entities in the Logical Design from which the table was derived.

The table definition must include the primary key of each table, as well as any other table-level constraints such as foreign keys and the tables which they reference.

## Columns

The column specification must include each column in each entity, with a textual description of the attribute that the column is intended to model. The column specification should also contain the datatype, rule, default, constraint, and nullability characteristics of the column.

## Indexes

The index specification should describe an initial indexing strategy, based on projected join criteria, transaction volume, and transaction frequency. The index specification should include the table name, columns involved, and unique constraint. It may also include a clustered or nonclustered index and fill factor.

 **Note**
While other portions of the Physical Database Design should not change during implementation and testing, the index specification will change through the testing phase. This is because while the performance characteristics of a DBMS may be deterministic, modeling all of the requisite factors is extremely difficult and time-consuming.

You may need to have feedback from the integration-test and system-test phases before you can achieve an optimal indexing strategy.

## Triggers

The triggers section of the Physical Database Design document will specify the trigger logic for each table. It will specify the policy regarding primary-key updates, cascading key updates, and cascading deletes. In addition, it will specify the key relationships between the entities in the physical design and the constraints on *insert*s, *update*s, and *delete*s based on other table populations.

For systems with a homogeneous approach to referential integrity, trigger-generation software can decrease development and maintenance time.

For systems which will be implemented using the ANSI IEF syntax (SQL Server 10.x), integrity constraints may be specified in the table definitions. However, triggers will continue to be required to implement complicated domain constraints and complicated business rules.

# Rules

The set of rules is the physical instantiation of the valid system domains. You can express rules as ranges, lists, regular expressions (picture strings) or tell whether the rule is to be bound to a particular datatype(s) or column(s).

In SQL Server 10.x, you can also implement rules as column or table constraints.

# Views

The set of views must be specified, including the data items that will be viewed and the criteria constraining the view.

Views add complexity to a data model. Use views primarily to restrict access in an ad hoc querying environment.

Stored procedures provide the benefits of views without the negative implications.

# Default

The default specification must contain the list of all default values to be used in the system. The default specification should tell whether the default will be bound to user-defined datatype(s) or column(s).

In SQL Server 10.x, you can also implement defaults as column constraints.

# User-defined datatypes

Each user-defined datatype will be specified along with its system datatype, default, rule, and nullability.

User-defined datatypes are for scenarios where a number of columns will share the same system datatype, rule, and possibly default. They should not be used in place of system datatypes.

## Integrity

In SQL Server 10.x, you can design in several ways. You can use the integrity specification to describe integrity constraints for tables and columns in the physical database design. The specification should include items such as:

- unique constraint
- primary key
- foreign-key references policy (cascade/restrict)
- primary-key update policy (cascade/restrict)
- domain constraints

If the target database is SQL Server 10.x or higher, the specification may include a recommendation as to how to implement a particular integrity constraint. For example, a foreign-key restriction may be implemented using triggers or using a foreign-key constraint on the table definition. Domain constraints may be implemented using a combination of rules and user-defined datatypes, or using IEF syntax in the table definition.

## Security

The security specification must contain information necessary to produce *grant* statements and will include lists of users, columns, tables, and views that will be restricted.

In SQL Server 10.x, the security specification may also include users and roles.

## Pre-engineered data

The Pre-engineered Data specification must list any data that will be deployed with the system. This data will include reference-table values, seeding values (for monotonic keys), and configuration data.

## Segments and devices

Initial physical-allocation strategies of tables and indexes to segments and devices must be specified in this section.

# Appendix E
## *Naming Guidelines*

*The purpose of this appendix is to provide broadly-applicable naming guidelines for use with SYBASE SQL Server. The guidelines may be used "as is," or as the basis for building specialized naming standards.*

Naming guidelines are presented for eighteen distinct and persistent SQL Server and database components. This appendix uses the general term "object" to refer to these components, though not all of their definitions are stored in the *sysobjects* table. The names are presented in the same order that you might create the objects. Naming guidelines are also presented for the scripts that must be written and maintained to create those objects.

The guidelines provide names that are:

- readable
- consistent
- extensible
- durable

The conventions were derived from standards developed and used on Sybase Worldwide Professional Services projects in North America and Europe.

## General guidelines for naming

This handbook presents conventions that are meaningful and descriptive, and include some information about the objects' essential properties.

Though SQL Server's system tables provide information about the objects it maintains, objects are often referred to in other contexts: in phone calls, on white-boards, in documents, in e-mail, and on diagrams. By embedding a small amount of information about an object in its name, you can avoid ambiguity.

Use complete words wherever possible. Avoid all but standard abbreviations, and don't try to keep an object name arbitrarily short to save keystrokes. Names are all lower case.

# Conventions

Naming guidelines—for both objects and the scripts that are written to create the objects—are presented as templates composed of one or more of the following:

- underscores—the elements of a name are separated by underscores for improved readability,
- substitutions—represented by italicized characters, indicating that the element is composed of characters provided by the user,
- constants—represented by roman type (non-italicized) characters,
- ellipses—indicate that the name-element may vary in length, and
- brackets—indicate that the enclosed character is included only under specific conditions, as defined in the guideline.

For example, the naming for triggers is presented as:

**trg_[d][i][u]_*ttttt*...**

- The roman type prefix of the name ("trg_") is a constant; all trigger names will begin with this string.
- The underscores demarcate the name's three elements.
- The brackets around the characters "d," "i," and "u" indicate that you will include these characters based upon the criteria presented in the guideline.
- The italicized characters "*ttttt*" indicate that you will substitute appropriate words or strings for the italicized text.
- The ellipsis in the third element indicates that this element can be of varying length.

Script names are presented similarly. The constant elements in scripts' names correspond to the underlying Transact-SQL commands used to create the object. All script names end with the ".sql" suffix.

# Examples

Each of the guidelines presented includes a set of examples to illustrate use of the templates. These examples all refer to a physical design for a hypothetical travel agency using Sybase. The design has one database for business operations and one database for tracking customer travel information. There are servers in New York and Paris. The objects described in the examples concentrate on employee information, air carrier information, and group travel program information.

# SQL Server identifier requirements _____

All of the names you compose with these guidelines must conform to the rules for identifiers given in *SYBASE SQL Server Reference Manual—Vol. I*. Here are a few reminders:

- Identifiers can be a maximum of 30 bytes in length, whether or not multibyte characters are used.
- Names may begin with alphabetic characters, the @ symbol, the # symbol, or an underscore.
- Reserved words may only be used if names are enclosed in double quotation marks.

# Servers

## Compose server names in the form:

> *hhhhh..._ttt_vvvvv...*, where
>> *hhhhh...* identifies the host or machine name,
>>
>> *ttt* represents the type of server, for example,
>>
>>> **sql**      (SQL Server)
>>>
>>> **bkp**     (backup server)
>>>
>>> **rep**      (replication server)
>>
>> *vvvvv...* represents the version of the server, such as:
>>
>>> **dev**     (development)
>>>
>>> **test**     (testing)
>>>
>>> **prod**    (production).

## Consider these examples:

> nysparc_sql_prod
>
> nysparc_sql_test
>
> nysparc_bkp_prod
>
> paris_rep_dev

## Add servers with a script:

> **add_servers_hhhhh....sql,** where
>> *hhhhh...* is the host or machine name, and
>>
>> **.sql** is the script suffix.
>
> Create servers for a host in a single script.

## Keep in mind:

> You can assign server names when installing SQL Server for the first time, or with the *sp_addserver* procedure.

# Database Devices

## Compose database device names in the form:

**dev_*xxx*_*n*,** where

> **dev** is a constant indicating that the object is a database device,
>
> ***xxx*** indicates the use of the device, either
>
> > **log** for transaction logs or
> >
> > **dat** for data and indexes, and
>
> ***n*** is a sequential number corresponding to the *vdevno* value specified in the *disk init* command.

## Consider these examples:

> dev_dat_1
> dev_dat_2
> dev_log_1

## Create devices with a script:

**disk_init_*sssss*....sql,** where

> ***sssss...*** is the SQL Server name, and
>
> **.sql** is the script suffix.

Database devices for a SQL Server should be created in a single script.

## Keep in mind:

Device names are unique for a SQL Server.

The *disk init* command establishes the relationship between a physical operating system disk resource and a database device.

If you are using mirroring, give names to the mirror devices that correspond to the primary database device names. For example, when setting up mirroring of the database device *dev_dat_1*, name the operating system disk resource *dev_dat_1_mir*.

# Dump Devices_____

## Compose dump device names in the form:

**dmp_*ddddd..._uuu*,** where
> **dmp** is a constant indicating that the device is for dumps,
> *ddddd...* is the database name, and
> *uuu* indicates the use of the device:
>> **db** for database dumps, or
>> **log** for transaction log dumps.

## Consider these examples:

> dmp_travel_test_log
> dmp_travel_test_db
> dmp_operations_prod_log
> dmp_operations_prod_db

## Add dump devices with a script:

**add_dump_devices_*sssss*....sql,** where
> *sssss...* is the SQL Server name, and
> **.sql** is the script suffix.

All dump devices for a SQL Server should be created in a single script.

## Keep in mind:

The *sp_addumpdevice* stored procedure establishes the relationship between a physical operating system disk resource and a dump device. The parameters specify the physical file name or the type of device (tape or disk).

Dump device names must be unique for a SQL Server.

# Segments

## *Compose segment names in the form:*

**seg_*n***, where

**seg** is a constant indicating that the object is a segment, and

***n*** is a sequential identifier beginning with 1.

## *Consider these examples:*

seg_1

seg_2

seg_3

## *Add segments with a script:*

**add_segments_*ddddd*....sql**, where

***ddddd...*** is the name of the database, and

**.sql** is the script suffix.

This script is used to create the segments, and must be maintained as segments are extended.

## *Keep in mind:*

Segment names must be unique to a database.

Segments can shared by many objects of different types, and objects are often moved or extended throughout the life of a database. Descriptive names are not used for segments because they would not be readable or durable.

# Databases _____

## Compose database names in the form:

> *ddddd..._vvvvv...*, where
>> *ddddd...* is a descriptive and meaningful name, and
>> *vvvvv...* is a descriptive and meaningful indication of the version, environment, or use of the database. Examples include:
>>> **dev**     (development)
>>> **test**    (testing)
>>> **acpt**    (acceptance or system testing)
>>> **prod**    (production)
>>> **train**   (training)

## Consider these examples:

> travel_dev
> travel_test
> operations_prod

## Create databases with scripts:

> **create_database_*ddddd*....sql**, where
>> *ddddd...* is the database name, and
>> **.sql** is the script suffix.
>
> Each database should be created in a separate script.
>
> The database script contains Transact-SQL commands to:
> - create the database,
> - create transaction log, and
> - assign database owner.

## Keep in mind:

> Database names must be descriptive and meaningful. Database names may be up to 30 characters long and must be unique on a SQL Server.

# Rules_____

## Compose rule names in the form:

**rul_*xxxxx*...**, where

**rul** is a constant indicating that the object is a rule, and

***xxxxx*...** is a descriptive name.

## Consider these examples:

rul_branch_number
rul_employee_number
rul_carrier_id

## Create rules with a script:

**create_rules_*ddddd*....sql**, where

***ddddd*...** is the database name, and

**.sql** is the script suffix.

All rules for a database should be created by a single script.

This script should include the Transact-SQL commands necessary to create all rules in the database. Each rule must be created in its own batch (i.e., end with a *go* statement).

## Keep in mind:

Rule names for each owner must be unique in a database. Rule names may be up to 30 characters long.

# Defaults _____

## Compose default names in the form:

> **def_*xxxxx*...**,where
>> **def** is a constant indicating that the object is a default, and
>> ***xxxxx*...** is a descriptive name.

## Consider these examples:

> def_country
> def_meal_code
> def_commission_percentage

## Create defaults with a script:

> **create_defaults_*ddddd*....sql**, where
>> ***ddddd*...** is the database name, and
>> **.sql** is the script suffix
>
> This script should include the Transact-SQL commands necessary to create all defaults in the database.

## Keep in mind:

> Each default must be created in its own batch (i.e., end with a *go* statement). Default names for each owner must be unique in a database.

# User-defined datatypes _____

## Compose user-defined datatype names in the form:

**typ_*ss*_*xxxxx*...,** where

**typ** is a constant indicating that the object is a user-defined datatype,

*ss* is a code representing the SQL Server system datatype upon which the user-defined datatype is built, and

*xxxxx*... is a descriptive name.

Refer to the system datatypes in Table E.1.

## Consider these examples:

typ_ch_carrier_id
typ_in_branch_number
typ_sm_rebate

## Add user-defined datatypes with a script:

**add_types_*ddddd*....sql,** where

*ddddd*... is the database name, and

**.sql** is the script suffix.

All datatypes in a database should be maintained in a single script.

This script should include the Transact-SQL commands necessary to

* add each datatype using *sp_addtype*,
* bind *rule*s to datatypes ( if necessary), and
* bind *default*s to datatypes (if necessary).

## Keep in mind:

Datatype names must be unique in a database, however there may be datatypes with different names and the same definition.

Table E.1 lists possible system datatype codes to use in naming user-defined datatypes.

Table E.1 Recommended Codes for Sybase System Datatypes ------------------

| CODE | Sybase system type |
|------|--------------------|
| in | *int* |
| si | *smallint* |
| ti | *tinyint* |
| nm | *numeric* |
| dc | *decimal* |
| fl | *float* |
| re | *real* |
| dp | *double precision* |
| mo | *money* |
| sm | *smallmoney* |
| ch | *char* |
| vc | *varchar* |
| bi | *binary* |
| vb | *varbinary* |
| bt | *bit* |
| dt | *datetime* |
| sd | *smalldatetime* |
| tx | *text* |
| im | *image* |

# Columns_____

## Compose column names in the form:

*aaaaa..._aaaaa..._aaaaa...,* where

> *aaaaa...* are descriptive and meaningful singular nouns, separated by underscores, that refer to the logical *attribute(s)* the column represents.

## Consider these examples:

employee_number
carrier_id
destination

## Define columns with scripts:

**create_table_*ttttt*....sql,** where

> *ttttt...* is the table name, and
> **.sql** is the script suffix.

Columns are assigned names when the table is created or altered.

Each table in a database should be created in its own script.

## Keep in mind:

Column names should be fully descriptive; an untrained observer should be able to determine what the column name denotes without special knowledge.

Always assign identical names to columns that will be used in primary-key/foreign-key relationships.

For example, in Figure E.1, *platform_name* is assigned as the name of the primary key of the *hardware_platform* table and as a foreign key in the *application* table. The column names are identical.

Use abbreviations sparingly, preferably from a well-maintained and approved list.

Column names must be unique within a table and there may be up to 250 columns per table. Column names may be up to 30 characters long.

Figure E.1 Column naming example --------------------------------------------------------

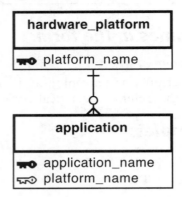

# Constraints_____

## Compose constraint names in the form:

*ttt*_[c]_*xxxxx*..., where

*ttt* represents the type of constraint,

**chk** for check constraints,

**unq** for unique constraints,

**pky** for primary key constraints,

**c** represents a constant included if the constraint is implemented as a *clustered index* (omitted if nonclustered, not applicable for check constraints), and

*xxxxx*... describes the nature of the constraint or column(s) upon which the constraint is applied.

## Consider these examples:

pky_c_carrier_id
unq_employee_number
unq_c_flight_number
chk_meal_code

## Define constraints with a script:

**create_table_*ttttt*....sql** where

*ttttt*... is the table name, and

**.sql** is the script suffix.

Constraints are assigned names when the table is created. Each table in a database should be created in its own script.

## Keep in mind:

SQL Server creates indexes to enforce *unique* and *primary key* constraints. These indexes will take the constraint name you specify in the *create table* statement. The constraint-type prefix enables you to quickly identify the indexes that are constraint-related when viewing the output from *sp_help*.

# Tables

## Compose table names in the form:

*eeeee..._eeeee..._eeeee...*, where

> *eeeee...* are descriptive and meaningful singular nouns, separated by underscores, that refer to the logical *entity(ies)* the table represents.

## Consider these examples:

air_segment
payment
group_client
employee

## Create tables with scripts:

**create_table_*ttttt*....sql** where

> *ttttt...* is the table name, and
>
> **.sql** is the script suffix.

Each table in a database should be created in its own script.

This script should include the Transact-SQL commands to:

- create the table,
- specify all columns, including datatype and null status,
- bind rules to columns (if not bound to datatypes),
- bind defaults to columns (if not bound to datatypes),
- define primary keys with *sp_primarykey*,
- define foreign keys with *sp_foreignkey*, and
- specify column or table constraints.

## Keep in mind:

Table names should be fully descriptive; an untrained observer should be able to determine what the table name denotes without special knowledge.

Use abbreviations sparingly, preferably from a well-maintained and approved list.

Table names for each owner must be unique within a database.

# Indexes

## Compose index names in the form:

**idx_[u][c]_***ttttt...***_n,** where

> **idx** is a constant indicating that the object is an index,
>
> **u** is a constant indicating a *unique index* (otherwise omitted),
>
> **c** is a constant indicating a *clustered index* (otherwise omitted).
>
> ***ttttt...*** is the name of the table referred to by the index, and
>
> ***n*** is a sequential identifier, where
>
> > **1** indicates the index on the primary key, and
> >
> > **2** and up are used for all other indexes.

## Consider these examples:

> idx_uc_air_segment_1 (a unique, clustered index on the primary key of the *air_segment* table)
>
> idx_group_client_2 (a non-unique, nonclustered index on the *group_client* table)

## Create indexes with scripts:

**create_indexes_***ttttt....***sql,** where

> ***ttttt...*** is the table name, and
>
> **.sql** is the script suffix.

All indexes for a single table should be created in a single script.

This script should include the SQL commands necessary to:

- create the clustered index (if there is a clustered index), and
- create the non-clustered indexes.

## Keep in mind:

Index names should convey important properties and refer to the name of the table.

There may be only 1 clustered index per table and up to 250 nonclustered indexes per table with a maximum of 250 total indexes (clustered and nonclustered) per table. Index names must be unique for a table and may be up to 30 characters long. In a case where the table name is longer than 21 characters, the table name should be abbreviated from right to left attempting to keep the beginning as close to the table name as possible. This will assist in querying database objects.

It may be useful to create and maintain a script to drop all indexes on a table, for example before loading table data with **bcp**. Such a script file should be named:

**drop_indexes_*ttttt*....sql,** where

    *ttttt...* is the table name, and

    **.sql** is the script suffix.

This script should include the SQL commands necessary to drop all indexes for a given table.

# Views

## Compose view names in the form:

**vw_*xxxxx*..._*xxxxx*...,** where

**vw** is a constant indicating that the object is a view, and

*xxxxx*... are descriptive and meaningful singular nouns, separated by underscores, that refer to the tables, columns, or rows the view represents.

## Consider these examples:

vw_employee_review

vw_group_statistics

vw_carrier_rebate

## Create views with scripts:

**create_view_*vvvvv*....sql,** where

*vvvvv*... is the view name, and

**.sql** is the script suffix.

Each view in a database should be created in its own script.

This script should include the Transact-SQL commands necessary to create the view.

## Keep in mind:

The *vw* prefix will distinguish a *view* from a *table* and alert a developer to the existence of the Transact-SQL code hidden by the view, and to the restrictions on inserting and updating through a view.

The view name should match the name of the entity(ies) it represents as closely as possible.

Each column in a view must be named with a descriptive name. Use the base column name whenever possible.

# Triggers

## *Compose trigger names in the form:*

**trg_[d][i][u]_*ttttt*...**, where

**trg** is a constant indicating that the object is a trigger,

**d** indicates the trigger is defined for *delete* (otherwise the character is omitted),

**i** indicates the trigger is defined for *insert* (otherwise the character is omitted),

**u** indicates the trigger is defined for *update* (otherwise the character is omitted), and

***ttttt*...** is the name of the affected table.

## *Consider these examples:*

trg_iu_air_segment

trg_d_group_client

trg_i_employee

## *Create triggers with scripts:*

**create_triggers_*ttttt*....sql**, where

***ttttt*...** is the table name, and

**.sql** is the script suffix.

All triggers for a single table should be maintained in a single script. This script should include the Transact-SQL commands necessary to create the trigger(s) for the table.

## *Keep in mind:*

The constant prefix in the trigger name helps you differentiate triggers from stored procedures when using *sp_depends*.

# Stored Procedures

## Compose stored procedure names in the form:

**proc_*aaaaa..._xxxxx...*,** where

**proc** is a constant indicating that the object is a procedure,

*aaaaa...* indicates the main action or the business rule implemented by the stored procedure, and

*xxxxx...* gives the name(s) of the objects upon which the procedure is carried out, as meaningful as possible.

## Consider these examples:

proc_get_carrier

proc_add_group_client

proc_validate_air_segment

proc_transfer_employee

## Create stored procedures with scripts:

**create_procedure_*ppppp...* sql,** where

*ppppp...* is the procedure name, and

**.sql** is the script suffix.

Each stored procedure in a database should be created in its own script. This script should include the SQL commands necessary to drop and recreate the stored procedure.

## Keep in mind:

The name of a stored procedure must be meaningful in order to facilitate reading the source code that executes the procedure.

# Logins

## Compose login names in the form:

*f[m]lllll...*, where
> *f* is the first letter of the user's first name,
> *m* is the user's middle initial (if necessary to prevent duplicates), and
> *lllll...* is the user's last name.

## Consider these examples:

| | |
|---|---|
| lkampinsky | (Leon Kampinsky) |
| mjimenez | (Mercedes Jiménez) |
| jjrousseau | (Jean Jacques Rousseau) |
| jprousseau | (Jean Pierre Rousseau) |

## Add logins with a script:

**add_logins_*sssss*....sql**, where
> **sssss...** is the server name, and
> **.sql** is the script suffix.

All SQL Server login definitions should be maintained in a single script. The script to create the SQL server logins includes Transact-SQL commands to add each login, with password and default database.

## Keep in mind:

A SQL Server login account is used to control a connection to the SQL Server. A login account is represented by a login name/password combination. When possible, define SQL Server login names (using the *sp_addlogin* stored procedure) the same as the operating system username. This eliminates the need for the user to re-enter a user name when connecting to a SQL Server.

Login names must be unique within a SQL Server and may be up to 30 characters in length. A password is also assigned at login creation time. The user may change the assigned password with the *sp_password* stored procedure.

At the time a login is defined, a default database may also be assigned. It is recommended that a default database other than *master* be assigned for every user.

# Groups _____

## Compose group names in the form:

*xxxxx..._xxxxx...*, where

> *xxxxx...* are descriptive and meaningful words, separated by underscores, that refer to the functional group.

## Consider these examples:

agent
marketing
manager
accounting

## Add groups with a script:

**add_groups_*ddddd*....sql**, where

> *ddddd...* is the database name, and
>
> **.sql** is the script suffix.

All the groups in a database should be maintained in a single script.

This script should include the Transact-SQL commands necessary to add each group and assign command permissions to each group.

## Keep in mind:

Group names should be descriptive and meaningful; they must be unique within a database and may be up to 30 characters in length.

# Users

## Compose database user names in the form:

*f[m]lllll...*, where
    *f* is the first letter of the user's first name,
    *m* is the user's middle initial (if necessary to prevent duplicates), and
    *lllll...* is the user's last name

## Consider these examples:

| | |
|---|---|
| lkampinsky | (Leon Kampinsky) |
| mjimenez | (Mercedes Jiménez) |
| jjrousseau | (Jean Jacques Rousseau) |
| jprousseau | (Jean Pierre Rousseau) |

## Add database users with a script:

**add_users_*ddddd*....sql**, where
    *ddddd...* is the database name, and
    **.sql** is the script suffix.
All the users in a database should be created in a single script.
This script should include the SQL commands necessary to:
- add each user to the database,
- assign each user to a group, and
- grant permissions to each user.

## Keep in mind:

Make database user names the same as the SQL Server login account name. Users are added to a database with the *sp_adduser* system procedure. Database user names must be unique within a database and may be up to 30 characters in length. At the time of user definition the SQL Server login account must have been defined. Also, the database user may be assigned to an existing group.

# Summary of Object Names

Table E.2 summarizes all of the object types and their suggested names.

**Table E.2 Summary of Object Names** --------------------------------------------------------------

| Object Type | Object Name | Example |
|---|---|---|
| column | *aaaaa..._aaaaa..._aaaaa...* | employee_number |
| constraint | *ttt_*[c]*_xxxxx...* | pky_c_carrier_id |
| database | *ddddd..._vvvvv...* | travel_dev |
| database device | dev_*xxx_n* | dev_dat_1 |
| datatype | typ_ss_*xxxxx...* | typ_ch_carrier_id |
| default | def_*xxxxx...* | def_country |
| dump device | dmp_*ddddd..._uuu* | dmp_travel_test_log |
| group | *xxxxx..._xxxxx...* | marketing |
| index | idx_[u][c]_*ttttt..._n* | idx_uc_air_segment_1 |
| login | *f*[m]*lllll...* | lkampinsky |
| rule | rul_*xxxxx...* | rul_branch_number |
| segment | seg_*n* | seg_1 |
| server | *hhhhh..._ttt_vvvvv...* | nysparc_sql_prod |
| stored procedure | proc_*aaaaa..._xxxxx...* | proc_get_carrier |
| table | *eeeee..._eeeee..._eeeee...* | group_client |
| trigger | trg_[d][i][u]_*ttttt...* | trg_iu_air_segment |
| user | *f*[m]*lllll...* | lkampinsky |
| view | vw_*xxxxx..._xxxxx...* | vw_employee_review |

# Appendix F
## *Glossary*

### Abstract key

a technique to effectively provide index capability for a *text* datatype column by adding a *varchar* column which contains keywords from the text column and creating an index on the value of the newly created column

### Aggregated data

in general, data composed from component data objects, or an entity composed of several attributes

### Artificial key

a primary key that serves only as an identifier and does not convey any further meaning. Typically, artificial keys have integer values which are maintained through a trigger, a stored procedure, or application software. Additionally, these values are often not exposed to system users. Synonyms: contrived key, surrogate key

### Associative table

a table that represents a "many-to-many" relationship, or a relationship of degree higher than two. The primary key of an associative table is usually the composite of two or more foreign keys.

### Attribute

a property of an entity which identifies, describes, or measures the entity and is of interest to the enterprise. It may be represented by one or more symbols.

## Automatic constraint

a referential integrity technique wherein the insertion of an unknown foreign key value automatically causes a new row with that value to be inserted in the primary table

## B-Tree

a storage structure for tables characterized by a dynamic index. The structure maintains information regarding a logical ordering of the table rows based on the values in one or more columns. Accesses to the table are resolved through the index, rather than the table itself.

## BLOB

Binary Large Object. This is non-ASCII, bit-oriented data which usually represents image data, or some other data which cannot be meaningfully represented in textual form.

## Cardinality

used without qualification, the term cardinality usually means maximum cardinality. Given a binary relationship **R** between entities **A** and **B**, the maximum cardinality of **R** indicates the maximum number of instances **a** which are related to a singe instance **b**, and conversely. Maximum cardinality is written as 1-1, 1-N, N-1, or M-N. Similarly, a minimum cardinality is specified as 0-0, 0-1, 1-0, or 1-1.

## Cascading constraint

a referential integrity technique wherein a primary key delete causes all rows with matching foreign keys to be automatically deleted. When these values are in turn primary keys, they may cause another set of foreign key rows to be deleted, in a cascading effect.

## Clustered index

an index in which the physical order and the logical (indexed) order is the same. The leaf level of a clustered index represents the data pages themselves.

## Column-wise vector

a relational design in which all values of a vector attribute are maintained in a single column

## Complex domain

a set of values for an attribute or column which relies on other data, complex business rules, or application-level information

## Composite index

an index composed of two or more columns

## Concurrency

controlled multiple and simultaneous uses of the data. Locking is the primary mechanism used to enforce protection of the data in concurrency to ensure data consistency and integrity.

## Contrived key

see Artificial key

## Cross-domain rule

a logical predicate which enforces domain integrity for a column or columns based on values from more than one domain (column)

## CRUD

Create Read Update Delete, permissions for users tracked in a chart referred to as a CRUD chart. This chart can also be used for transaction or business function analysis to identify data which is written but never read.

## DAC

Discretionary Access Control, a system of accesses to objects and commands which are granted and/or revoked at the discretion of a System Administrator or System Security Officer

## Data integrity

the correctness and completeness of data within a database

## Defaulting constraint

a referential integrity technique wherein the update or deletion of a primary key causes all matching foreign keys to be set to a default value

## Denormalization

the process of relaxing normal form representations of relationships. Denormalization is a major activity in transforming a logical database design to a physical representation, involving techniques such as storing redundant data, maintaining derived data, and collapsing tables.

## Derived column

a column whose value is a representation of some function performed on other columns' values

## Domain

the set of values which an attribute or column may assume. Allowable values may be specified either explicitly or implicitly with a logical predicate. Domains transform data into information.

## Domain integrity

the soundness of data values for a particular attribute or column. Domain integrity techniques include rules, defaults.

## Entity

a real-world thing of interest to the enterprise, represented by an identifying symbol. Typically, a logical entity will, at least initially, represent one table in a physical database design.

## Equijoin

a join based on equality

## ERD

Entity Relationship Diagram, a graphic modeling construct used to represent elements and their interrelationships with an emphasis on the state of the objects

## Exclusive lock

a SQL Server locking mechanism which holds a data page unavailable for read or write access except to the holder of the lock. It is associated with any write access to a data page and is always held for the duration of the surrounding transaction

## Fillfactor

a SQL Server configuration variable which determines how full SQL Server makes each page when creating a new index on existing data. The fillfactor percentage is used only at the time the index is created, and becomes less important the more changes to the data are made.

## Foreign key

an attribute or attributes of an entity which acts both as a descriptor and as a reference to occurrences of other entities. Its values are required to match the values of a primary key.

## Heap

a table whose physical ordering of rows is based on sequence of creation and updates. New row instances are always added to the end of the heap; row updates may or may not move the row to the end of the heap as well.

## Holdlock

a locking condition applied to a shared lock which holds the lock until the completion of a transaction versus completion of the read access

## Horizontal fragmentation

a technique for splitting tables, partitioning the rows of a table into disjoint subsets. The result is a set of tables with the same columns but with a different set of rows in each table.

## Identity

a SQL Server 10.x column definition which supports automatic generation of a unique, sequential number to identify a newly inserted row

## Index

a physical construct list of values for a column or columns, together with pointers to the locations of rows containing the values. Indexes are often but not always defined on primary and foreign keys. A clustered index also causes a physical re-ordering of the data rows based on the column values; a nonclustered index does not re-order the data rows.

## Indexable

the use of an index by the optimizer on a *where* clause which limits the number of page scans needed to satisfy a query. In such a case, the *where* clause is said to be indexable.

## Index covering

the ability to resolve an access to a data row simply by accessing its entry in a nonclustered index instance. This technique reduces access time since only the index page need be accessed, not the actual data page.

## Intra-row rule

a domain integrity constraint on one or more columns based on other columns' values within the row

## Join

a basic operation in a relational system. A join links the rows in two or more tables by comparing the values in specified columns.

## Junction table

see Associative table

## Leaf page

a page in an index that represents the nearest maintained reference to the actual data values. In a clustered index, the data pages are the leaf pages of the index. In a nonclustered index, there is an index page which acts as the leaf page, holding a pointer to a particular data page and a particular data row for each entry on the page.

## Least privilege

a policy for providing user privileges that stipulates that users and processes be granted only those accesses they need to perform their job or assigned business functions

## MAC

Mandatory Access Control, a means for granting or denying access to data and commands based strictly on the credentials of the user and the classification of the data and commands

## Mutually exclusive rule

a domain logic predicate which prohibits the existence of a value in one column if a value exists in another column. Mutual exclusion often occurs in single supertype table.

## Mutually inclusive rule

a domain logic predicate which requires the existence of a value in a column if a value exists in another column

## Nonclustered index

an index which maintains a logical ordering of data rows without altering the physical ordering of the rows

## Normalization

the process that eliminates data element redundancy by separating a database into groups of similar data. The major normal forms (first through fifth) do not address inter-table redundancies, just intra-table redundancies. The process typically involves nonloss decomposition, where a table is decomposed into two or more smaller tables by projection. All tables are in first normal form by definition.

## Nullifying constraint

a referential integrity technique wherein all matching foreign key values are set to null when the primary key is updated or deleted. This works only in situations where null is explicitly allowed in the foreign-key column.

## OAM

Object Allocation Map, an SQL Server accounting structure for tracking page allocations associated with a particular object

## Overindexing

applying indexes to a table where neither transaction analysis nor benchmarking has proven the usefulness/need for the indexes. In such cases, the index will only needlessly degrade *update* and *delete* operations without appropriately improving the query operations.

## Ownership chain

the hierarchy of users which own an object and all of its "container" objects such as the owner of a stored procedure, the owner of the table upon which the stored procedure operates, and the owner of the database which holds the table

## Page contention

more than one process or user trying to obtain a lock on a particular data page or index page in order to perform either a read or a write access function on the page

## Primary key

an attribute or attributes which act as a unique identifier for an entity instance

## Redundant column

a column value from one table repeated in a column in another table. Redundancy often improves performance on *select* operations, but degrades performance on *update* and can lead to data inconsistency.

## Referential integrity

an integrity rule in the relational model requiring that a foreign key which identifies the primary key of table **T** must either (1) be wholly null, or (2) match the primary key of some row in **T**

## Relationship

a verb or verb phrase, determined by business actions and rules, which represents the natural join between two entities. An occurrence of a relationship exists between one or more occurrences of the two entities.

## Restrictive constraint

a referential integrity technique wherein no foreign-key value can be inserted or deleted if no corresponding primary-key value exists in the associated table. Can also prohibit deletion of a primary key value as long as there are any matching foreign keys.

## Row-wise vector

a relational design in which a separate column is allocated for each value of a vector attribute

## SARG

Search Argument, a column used as a search argument in a *where* clause of a *select* statement

## Sequence number

a one-up number used as a surrogate key value for a row upon insertion into a table

## Sequence rule

a logic predicate on a domain which states that a value is only valid after a particular sequence of events has preceded it

## Shared lock

an SQL Server locking mechanism held for read access of a data page which allows other read accesses but no write accesses. Typically, the lock is held only while the page is being accessed and does not remain for the duration of the surrounding transaction unless a holdlock is indicated in the *select* syntax.

## Subtype

a subset of an entity referred to as a supertype. A subtype entity typically contains a unique subset of the supertype attributes, disjoint from the other subtypes of the supertypes.

## Supertype

an entity which represents a general categorization of a set of subtypes. The supertype entity contains all the attributes which are common to all the subtypes.

## Surrogate key

see Artificial key

## Table collapsing

a denormalization technique which combines logically distinct entities into one physical table in order to improve performance.

## Table splitting

a denormalization technique which partitions a logical entity into two or more physical tables in order to improve performance. Splitting may be horizontally, vertically, or mixed.

## Transaction

a mechanism for ensuring that a set of actions is treated as a single unit of work

## Transaction analysis

a study of the query patterns and entity accesses of a given logical representation of a data model. This analysis is vital in determining which physical constraints and which indexing should be applied when creating the physical representation of the database. Continued transaction analysis on the physical representation leads to the most effective design.

# Trigger

a special form of stored procedure that goes into effect when a user gives a change command such as *insert*, *delete*, or *update* to a specified table or column. Triggers are often used to enforce referential integrity.

# Update in place

a highly restricted update operation wherein a row may be altered without causing the row to be deleted and then re-inserted. The row then maintains its current position within the data page. This is a difficult standard to meet and typically requires sacrificing other physical design benefits in order to be achieved.

# Vector data

a plural attribute of an entity in which the number of values is constant for all entity instances

# Vertical fragmentation

a technique for splitting tables which partitions the columns of a table. Each fragment must include the primary key of the rows of the table.

# *Index*